ARCHITECTURAL DESIGN

EDITORIAL OFFICES:
42 LEINSTER GARDENS, LONDON W2 3AN
TEL: 071-402 2141 FAX: 071-723 9540

EDITOR: Maggie Toy
EDITORIAL TEAM: Iona Spens,
Katherine MacInnes, Mark Lane
ART EDITOR: Andrea Bettella
CHIEF DESIGNER: Mario Bettella
DESIGNER: Laurence Scelles

CONSULTANTS: Catherine Cooke, Terry
Farrell, Kenneth Frampton, Charles Jencks,
Heinrich Klotz, Leon Krier, Robert Maxwell,
Demetri Porphyrios, Kenneth Powell, Colin
Rowe, Derek Walker

SUBSCRIPTION OFFICES:
UK: VCH PUBLISHERS (UK) LTD
8 WELLINGTON COURT, WELLINGTON STREET
CAMBRIDGE CB1 1HZ
TEL: (0223) 321111 FAX: (0223) 313321

USA AND CANADA: VCH PUBLISHERS INC
303 NW 12TH AVENUE DEERFIELD BEACH,
FLORIDA 33442-1788 USA
TEL: (305) 428-5566 / (800) 367-8249
FAX: (305) 428-8201

ALL OTHER COUNTRIES:
VCH VERLAGSGESELLSCHAFT MBH
BOSCHSTRASSE 12, POSTFACH 101161
69451 WEINHEIM
FEDERAL REPUBLIC OF GERMANY
TEL: 06201 606 148 FAX: 06201 606 184

Architectural Design is published six times per year (Jan/Feb; Mar/
Apr; May/Jun; Jul/Aug; Sept/Oct; and Nov/Dec). Subscription rates for
1994 (incl p&p): Annual subscription price: UK only £65.00, World DM
195, USA $135.00 for regular subscribers. Student rate: UK only
£50.00, World DM 156, USA $105.00 incl postage and handling
charges. Individual issues: £14.95/DM 39.50 (plus £2.30/DM 5 for
p&p, per issue ordered), US $24.95 (incl p&p).
Application to mail at second-class postage rates is pending at
Deerfield Beach, FL. Postmaster. Send address changes to Architectural Design, 303 NW 12th Avenue, Deerfield Beach, FL 33442-
1788. Printed in Italy.Origination by Print-Tek London. All prices
are subject to change without notice. [ISSN: 0003-8504]

CONTENTS

ARCHITECTURAL DESIGN **MAGAZINE**

Guy **Battle** *& Christopher* **McCarthy** *Interactive Urbanism • Maxwell* **Hutchinson** *Donald Trump • Nigel* **Reading** *Dynamical Symmetries • And Here's One I Designed Earlier •* **Arquitectonica** *Bank of Luxembourg Headquarters • Books • Academy Highlights • Exhibitions*

Arquitectonica, Bank of Luxembourg Headquarters, 1994. Photograph: Robin Barton

ARCHITECTURAL DESIGN **PROFILE** No 112

ARCHITECTURE AND FILM

Michael **Dear** *Between Architecture and Film • Murray* **Grigor** *Space in Time • Andrew* **Benjamin** *At Home with Replicants • Nikos* **Georgiadis** *Architectural Experience as Discourse of the (Un) Filmed • Kester* **Rattenbury** *Echo and Narcissus • François* **Penz** *Cinema and Architecture • Daniel* **Libeskind** *•* **Coop Himmelb(l)au** *•* **Schweitzer BIM** *• Hani* **Rashid** *& Lise Anne* **Couture** *• Elizabeth* **Diller** *+ Ricardo* **Scofidio** *• John C* **Hope** *•* **Westfourth Architecture PC** *• Brian* **Avery** *•* **Studio 333** *•* **Disney** *• Lorcan* **O'Herlihy**

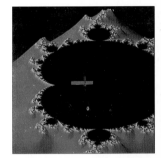

Detail of a Mandelbrot Set

The Fountainhead, 1949

GUY BATTLE AND CHRISTOPHER McCARTHY

MULTI-SOURCE SYNTHESIS
Interactive Urbanism

Singapore's new city Nah-Sing was first conceived in 2010 and all major infrastructure completed seven years later. It houses 10 million people and the city design incorporates energy and food production so that there is an overall surplus of energy, fed to the grid to feed the antique towns of the last century. Its designers remain unnamed, though databases record that they numbered 2,372,981. They mainly lived in Singapore, though contributions were also made from California and a group working from Weybridge in the UK. The systemic simulation at the core of the design process modelled city development over a 200 year period, and predicted an ideal decommission time of 137 years. The city's worldwide fame derives from the swathes of forest penetrating its plan, and the vibrant ecosystems that the forest sustains; an idea that is thought to have originated from the Weybridge group . . .

'The experts are all saying that our big cities have become ungovernable. What the hell do the experts know?'
Richard Daley, Mayor of Chicago, 1902-1976

Avant-garde technical revelations have projected our industry in leaps and bounds in a shroud of technical secrecy and public scepticism. We are notorious for the lack of unanimity this inspires between public and professionals. The public representatives are baffled by our need for change, and we are exasperated by the conservatism of bureaucrats who supposedly represent the views and interests of the public.

Over the last decade or more, the balance of power has shifted to the public from our profession still apologetic about the mistakes of 60s' master planning. Unfortunately our professionalism is too often described as arrogant, self-interested, and elitist. However we should take every possible route to reconcile directly with the public rather than through their agents. For example, technical progress may evolve by igniting the community's artistic and technical interest and abilities on a mass Utopian scale through the use of the new communication highways. Public participation would then utilise the complete creative spectrum of our industry as we attempt to solve the mystery of our built environment, in unison not in isolation.

If you were told that 5,000 people were killed travelling by air in the UK alone last year, you would seriously consider ever flying again. However, although 5,000 people were killed on the roads last year, that knowledge is unlikely to keep you from using your car. The reason is that we accept more risk if we are personally involved with decisions than if someone else is responsible – in other words, the acceptable concept of risk is relative to the level of personal involvement.

Architects and engineers are constantly urging the public to take risks and support innovation in the constant search for new solutions to old problems. Given the scale of the social and environmental problems now facing us, it would be difficult to deny that fearless innovation was necessary. Yet are we approaching the community with innovation in the wrong way? To even begin to deal with the environmental crisis, humanity needs to be decisive about technology and the design of the human environment. The necessary changes may seem outlandish and strange – and by taking them, we risk losing the familiarity and perceived utility of the status quo. Inertia sets in, and problems pile up unattended.

The only way to achieve a sustainable future is to involve the public in the design and decision-making process, in the most fundamental way. We need to make people more familiar with the macro-environmental and social issues which planners and architects and engineers face; invite them to make proposals and suggestions for change, and allow them to explore the consequences of their ideas. If the challenges and problems could be understood in this way then everyone could participate, sharing responsibility for urban policy and environmental change. Real innovation would become inevitable as we all progress together.

If this sounds unfeasible, it is only because we are not yet familiar with the tools necessary to facilitate this process. Most current public participation exercises are deeply unsatisfactory. To enable a radically different process, radically different tools are required; tools are now coming into existence in the shape of the computer programs SimCity, SimTower and

OPPOSITE: Boxer – urban design is presented as a fait accompli but its impact can not be underestimated; FROM ABOVE: Thermal satellite image of Merseyside – advanced information and image processing guides our new perception of human dwelling patterns; detail of St Helier, Jersey computer model – the simulated city is vibrant with industrial and commercial activities; babies – human interaction and communication provides a reason to live

SimEarth, written by the software house Maxis. The programs are the starting point for an entirely unpredicted approach in design; the first of a whole new generation of computer programs, giving a tantalising hint of future possibilities for architecture, urban design and many other fields.

Maxis

The co-founder and chief programmer for Maxis, Will Wright, is a self-taught Apple and Commodore programmer, driven by his fascination with statistics. He has brought sophisticated techniques such as simulation and adaptive computing to personal computer users in the form of a new generation of entertainment and learning software. Maxis' 'software toys' are so successful because of the programs' ability to make artificial life and simulation technologies accessible and entertaining. Individual components in the simulation follow simple rules, yet when combined with other components, exhibit complex processes that closely mirror real performance. Dynamic simulative computing thus becomes faster and more accessible, operating on ordinary personal computers (which are themselves constantly increasing in specification).

SimEarth, SimCity and SimTower are living simulation programs for desk-top computers, which enhance learning through visual exploration, experimentation and creativity with time. The simulations make learning enjoyable, because they develop ideas by trial and error. The user may create and instantly see the consequences of ideas; developments which may take hundreds or thousands of years on a global scale, decades on an urban scale and years on a building scale.

SimCity

SimCity provides an overview of the city in development, displaying a 3-D animated model in vivid colours. The user can 'zoom' in and out from an overview to close-up, make changes to street layouts or land-use patterns and watch the results. With only one finger the user can demolish buildings, draw new roads, change tax levels and build sewage plants, power stations and industrial areas.

In effect, the user becomes city designer and mayor, taking control of a city's construction and maintenance and assuming responsibility for everything from building energy management, air quality enforcement, tax collection and the encouragement of economic and social growth. Based on the designer's decisions, and governed by a set of complex algorithms, the city lives and grows, or decays and collapses. For instance, if pollution is too great, transport provision inadequate, or energy production

insufficient, then the city will not thrive. Month-by-month and year-by-year, SimCity updates the conditions of economy, society and city fabric in response to the prevailing conditions, providing a directly visual dynamic analysis which allows designers to look into, and speculate about, future developments.

SimCity is an excellent tool for learning and exploration, based on a process of trial and error with the reward, when proposals are successful, of watching the simulated city thrive. If taken a step further, the models can also be adapted to represent real cities, both existing and proposed. Major cities around the world, including London and Berlin, are presently being modelled, and Battle McCarthy is already using the program as a design tool on large-scale urban developments.

SimTower

SimTower, still under development by Maxis, involves a parallel process on a different scale, where the user becomes the architect, engineer and quantity surveyor for a building. Each change to the building's design in progress has impact on the energy consumption, budget, floor area and success of the building; changes which allow the designer to learn by trial and error, and create a resonant combination of factors. SimTower will help the user to develop an excellent understanding of the process of building design, and with algorithms based on real data should provide an essential sketch design tool for architects and engineers. SimTower will also be placeable within SimCity, extending even further the modelling and learning possibilities of the system.

SimEarth

SimEarth is nothing less than its name suggests – a planet simulation. Its basic premise is taken from James Lovelock's GAIA hypothesis, the classic theory suggesting that elements of the planet form a complex system which, seen from above, seems to be responsive and even self-regulating. SimEarth treats the planet as a complex system of the following interacting factors:
Chemical: atmospheric, composition and energy management
Geological: climate, continental drift, earthquakes
Biological: formation of life, form, evolution, food supply, biome types and distribution
Human: wars, civilisations, technology, waste control, pollution, food supply, energy supply.

The user's objective is to manage the earth by making use of the available data in the form of maps and graphics. The software constantly performs checks, calculations and updated testing of your plans and theories as you watch

OPPOSITE: Boy swinging – assured balance and cooperaton are essential as we reach for the future and cross the void into new hope: FROM ABOVE: Slums, Caracas; detail of Jerai International Park computer model showing data sheets; high street UK – the slums of Caracas, Venezuela and the high streets of Britain, data analysis and interactive simulation via modem enables the occupants of both to become part of the planning process and contribute to each others' well-being

v

the earth develop or decline. Of course, a truly accurate simulation of the climate has yet to be achieved by the most powerful super computers operated by the leading Met Offices of the world, and the accuracy of climate models will always be limited by the chaotic nature of fluid systems. SimEarth nevertheless provides an exploration of the basic principles and the opportunity to visualise possible outcomes of change. As a learning tool, whether to explore James Lovelock's GAIA hypothesis or the dynamic of atmospheric change, it is invaluable. And it does not require a leap of faith to imagine a SimEarth scenario consisting of cities modelled, designed and developed in SimCity and allowing the consideration of global trade along with the energy and resource balance.

Interactive Urbanism

Using these programs, anyone will soon be able to propose a building, place it in a city and observe the city's global impact, all in a day's work. And if that is the case, then that person is immediately empowered to take part in the design and decision-making process, allowing in its turn the re-definition of associated risk, and enabling the innovative and comprehensive planning of the worldwide changes necessary to combat the crises of environment and population growth.

A number of themes arise from the Maxis programs, as design aids to the community in their pursuit of improving the built environment:
(i) coordination and interrelation – the programs provide a means of integrating policy and investment, decision making to the complex and interrelated economic development, social policy (the reinforcement of social and economic cohesion), transportation and environment.
(ii) shared responsibility and participation – the programs encourage the acceptance of responsibility for the consequences of our action at all levels of the individual, the company and public administration, which is a fundamental prerequisite for environmental improvement. They emphasise the need for an understanding and knowledge of these consequences which are often so lacking, yet remind us that an informed choice does not discharge us from our responsibilities.
(iii) long-term objectives – the programs provide us with an insight into the future. They encourage long-term objectives well beyond the life span of the designer and work in favour of an attitude to using today's resources, which does not reduce their potential for future generations – the definition of sustainable development.

Pilot Projects

SimCity has sold over a million copies worldwide and is being used as child's game and for school projects. Battle McCarthy has been

pioneering its use in assisting in the design development of a number of major urban design projects such as Jerai International Park in Malaysia, and Palma New Town. As well as these new town and city projects, an island project has just started with Jersey Energy in the Channel Islands. This project first focused on the proposed 2 km² Water Front development which is to be constructed on reclaimed land adjacent to St Helier's harbour. The objective of the Island Project is to first involve the local participation for the design strategy for:

1	-	waterfront
2	-	harbour
3	-	town centre
4	-	parish of St Helier
5	-	all 12 parishes of the island

The first step is to install computers and touch screen displays at a number of public locations (the 'touch screen' facility makes it simple for people to interact with the computer, without worrying about mice or tablets – interfaces which not everyone is familiar with). Two versions of the St Helier model are provided showing the waterfront site with the proposed development and with a blank site. The public can therefore either amend the proposed scheme or propose their own ideas and see the consequences of their proposal take effect in front of them. Each proposal is recorded and sent back to a central design office for review. At the end of a two-week period, with the minimal investment of a few computers placed in public places, the design team has secured thousands of design ideas, and the people of the town have been given an enjoyable and entertaining opportunity to make a real contribution to the debate.

In stage two of the project, when the SimCity model is extended to the whole of the island, it will become a tool for the control of the environmental impact on the island. Because of commercial as well as environmental concerns, the local electricity company, Jersey Electricity, wants to avoid future expansion of power supply, but to maximise the return of the existing investment. SimCity provides an effective way of engaging public support and proposals on energy strategies for the island.

The island model, accessible from every Jersey household by modem, will enable users on Jersey to explore the parameters of domestic energy consumption, transport and power generation within a realistic model based on real data. Users will learn and understand about the importance of domestic energy-saving techniques and have the opportunity to explore, for instance, whether windfarms are a reasonable proposal in particular sites; along with other strategies for the island. Parishes and schools

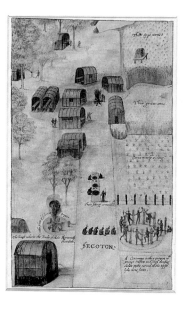

The village of Secoton, painted by John White, 1585-93 – lively interaction of people and the managed environment

will compete with each other for prizes; the challenge being to come up with the most environmentally sound and cost-effective energy proposal for Jersey.

Conclusions

Give a man a short-term lease on a garden, he will make it into a desert.
Give a long-term lease on a rock and he will make it into a garden.

To create a sustainable future, the working of the whole system must be considered, not just the separated parts: planet; continent; country; region; town. District neighbourhood and building must be considered at once. They must also be considered as dynamic systems over time, as we know that simple systems can quickly generate complex and chaotic behaviour. Computer programs such as SimEarth, SimCity and SimTower are simple, accessible and affordable tools which will revolutionise the design approach towards our built environment.

It is fundamental that invention becomes the mainstream of our culture if we are to find solutions to the growing problems which face us. These programs will allow people to understand and participate in the design and decision-making process, enlisting their support for necessary innovation. They exploit the opportunity of collective decision-making based on qualitative judgements and allow the exchange of information which yields the unexpected, even unsought answers from which true innovation results. By involving people in the processes of designing the future the programs give people a reason to live.

For the immediate future such initiatives will be complementary to the design process rather than replace it; the computer models are obviously simplifications, as are all models, and therein lies much of their utility. Nevertheless, with the continuing spread of information superhighways across the world and the developing subtlety of the programs, ever greater possibilities will open up, and the role of architects and engineers will continue to change. Mass communication using sophisticated tools like SimCity could create a new era of scientific, organisational, social and intellectual creativity.

The city's worldwide fame derives from the swathes of forest penetrating its plan, and the vibrant ecosystems that the forest sustains; an idea that is thought to have originated from the Weybridge group . . . though no one can be sure of this. For the individuals connected together on the net became as neurons in a brain; acting in response to each other in a complex and unpredictable process. Ideas fired from site to site, gaining or losing momentum and always modified and influenced by the interaction with other aspects of the developing masterplan . . . The design process took 12 months, though most designers did not remain connected for more than a month, moving on to other tasks as their interests and skills waxed and waned . . .

The authors would like to acknowledge the contribution made by Robert Webb to the preparation of this article.

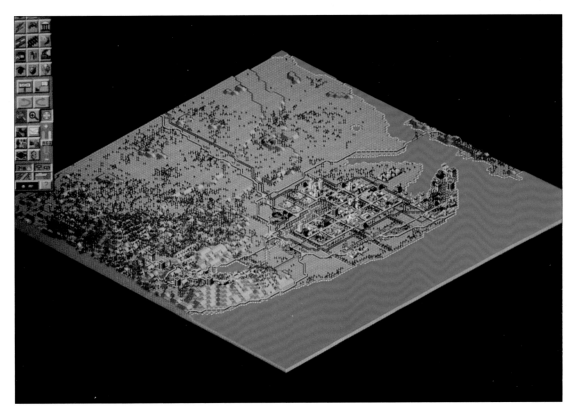

FROM ABOVE: Computer model of St Helier, Jersey, used in interactive planning exerise; Franz Kline in his studio – 'his pictures give the sense of too much pressure straining against too little space'; computer model of Jerai International Park, Malaysia – SimCity can empower the individual to understand and manipulate the urban environment

DONALD TRUMP
MAXWELL HUTCHINSON

P is for profit, prosperity, pomposity, pride and prejudice.
P is also for purpose, position, persuasion, privacy and patronage. Architectural patronage. T is for trouble, trial, tribulation, topicality, toughness, tenacity and tower.

As we near the end of the 20th century, there are few individual names which can be linked to great works of architecture. Who are the great architectural patrons who immediately spring to mind? Peter Palumbo and his obsession with James Stirling's building for Number One Poultry, now bringing the Victorian nonsense of Mappin and Webb crashing to the ground. Stuart Lipton, one of the few mandarins of British property whose name is linked to architecture of quality at Broadgate Arena and Stockley Park. Frank Lloyd Wright built houses for many a patron with a name: Fricke, Robie, Moore et al; and then of course The Guggenheim. David Mellor (him of kitchen fame) commissioned Michael and Patty Hopkins for a cutlery factory and an office building at Butler's Wharf. Dr Edith Farnsworth paid through the nose for Mies van der Rohe to build her one of the most famous houses of the 20th century.

But, all in all, individual named patrons of quality architecture are few and far between. Most architectural patronage hides behind the corporate veil; be it governmental, non-governmental or corporate.

The Seagram Building, the Johnson Wax Building, the Lloyds Building, the ITN Building in Grays Inn Road, Canary Wharf – all are the products of corporate patronage in one guise or another. When it comes to divining the nature of architectural patronage as the world gears itself up for the nuclear building spend on the millennium, how many individuals will stand up and put their name, their buck and their reputation behind a building more than a house a small factory or a personal jewel case?

Jump out of a yellow cab in New York City on an unusually fresh day around Easter and ask anyone who is prepared to pay the civility of an answer who is building New York today and the answer is plain and simple. The Rockefeller family built or at least catalysed, the centre of Manhattan as we know it today. The Reichman family beat a path to Battery Park at the south

end of the island, cheek by jowl with Wall Street. But who is the real estate maestro of Manhattan today? Who builds the icons that mean as much as the Chrysler and the Empire State? Watch your Ps and Ts and you'll find the answer. T is for tower and T is for Trump. P is for profit and D is for Donald. There is one name which shakes the foundations of New York real estate more than the San Francisco earthquake: one Donald J Trump. President of the Trump Organisation who according to Chen Sam and Associates Inc (a PR agency which coincidentally he shares with Elizabeth Taylor): '. . . is known world-wide as a developer *par excellence* of our era. His name is synonymous with an uncanny ability to see the unseen potential in everything from a non-descript parcel of land, to an uncommon structure, to a trend or style – and then bring that potential to life with enthusiasm, with originality and always with style. These attributes are at work in all aspects of Mr Trump's life – as a professional developer, a philanthropist, public celebrity, private man. The archetypal astute business man, the deal maker's deal maker, engaged citizen, sportsman – in all these roles, Mr Trump seeks standards of excellence while expanding his professional interests in real estate, gaming, sport and entertainment'.

So there. Hole in one. At the heart of all that little lot is little Donald, one of America's major personal patrons of architecture. The most obvious example is the glitziest addition to the south end of Fifth Avenue near Central Park, Trump Tower. A tourist trophy mandated on any Manhattan itinerary.

Trump Tower, his 58 storey block on the Central Park end of still hyper-fashionable Fifth Avenue is as much a New York attraction as the recently refurbished Guggenheim Museum which has made the long gone Frank Lloyd Wright this season's darling of the chattering classes. Wright's gallery interior, cool, classic and restrained as it is, is the height of architectural good taste even today, decades after its realisation. The entrance of *maison* Trump is like gate crashing Imelda Marcos' jewel case. But as Trump has it (and he does): 'The entrance which is all brass and very hard to maintain and all that . . . [is] very high grade and every expensive . . . It's a glizty entrance . . . [It's] what brings everybody in. It's like a lure. I wanted something

FROM ABOVE: Donald Trump 1990; Trump Tower, New York City, 1983; the site for the Riverside South development, New York City

that was going to be like a beacon.' In all honesty Trump Tower, at least as a pinnacle in the new Manhattan skyline, is no better, no worse and probably a little more admirable than some of the city's recent acquisitions.

The Tower was apparently designed by architect, Mr Scott, but Trump himself claims the credits for the atrium which packs in the punters like no other building since the Empire State.

This meeting with Donald Trump turned out to be an even more truncated chat than could have been expected, having dashed across the 'pond' simply for the chance to meet the capitalist icon whose net worth *Forbes Magazine* rated at around $1.7 billion in late 1989 – before he lost the Trump Shuttle airline, his 282 foot yacht the Trump Princess and the Trump Palm Beach condo. If that wasn't enough humiliation for Mr Manhattan, his assets chilled into a debt that swelled to around $1 billion. He may have settled with Ivana for a neat $10 million – cheap at the price thanks to a pre-nuptial agreement but he still keeps his bankers at arm's length.

His architect may have fashioned the envelope of Trump Tower and, to be fair, given it some subtlety in the way it turns the corner and manages some external terraces at higher level, but Donald claims all the plaudits for that atrium. 'I did the atrium. Let's put it this way, if I weren't involved in the design of Trump Tower there wouldn't be an atrium, it wouldn't look anything like it looks and it wouldn't work. The entrance would have been much narrower. I made this conscious decision to make it much wider and grander and more open. The entrance would have been narrower than it is – it wouldn't have been as grand as it is. And I just don't believe it would have worked.'

The conversation then went on to architectural values and the way in which a multi-billionaire spends his money on architecture, how he chooses the people with whom to work and the style which he feels will enliven America in the run up to the year 2000.

Early in the conversation he seemed to have his views cut and dried and, apparently, purposefully rooted in an individual sense of the progress of modernism.'I mean my preference is tower, modern, glass . . . . the Seagram Building, the Transco Building in Texas which I think is a great building. [I] tend to go tower, height, glass as opposed to the old fasioned, more traditional look. But I've done everything.'

But his view of the future of architecture seems to be utterly at odds with his preferences. When asked about the way in which architecture and design is going to develop in the 90s, in a new supposedly softer era where we are all meant to be calmer and more quiet, his reply went, literally, and in contrast to the assertive view of 20 percent of an hour ago, like this: 'I think it's going to take all shapes, now we're at the point where its taking all forms and all shapes. When Philip Johnson started from the modern to the old with the AT&T building, all of a sudden everyone was doing AT&T buildings, they were doing the old. Now people are doing everything: modern, post modern, old new, glass, brick, everything. I don't think there's gonna be one form any more. I don't think there's gonna be an age of this or an age of that. I think you're gonna have lots of different looks.'

So does Trump know his mind? Is he the ultimate post-modern pluralist patron? He certainly has a new wife and certainly continues to patronise the property industry and architects despite the turmoil of the last few years of his life.

The towering Trump magnetism recently attracted Henry Cheng, Managing Director of New World Development Company Limited and Vincent Lo, Chairman of Shui On Group, to form a multi-million dollar joint venture for the development of Riverside South, the last large undeveloped site in Manhattan. This history making deal reverses the overseas drain of dollars by bringing foreign investment to the United States on a grand scale. The Riverside South project comprises some 75 acres on the old Penn Station rail yards on Manhattan's West Side, encompassing the area from 59th to 72nd

FROM ABOVE: The Plaza Hotel, New York City, 1988; Trump Plaza Hotel and Casino, Atlantic City, New Jersey, 1984; proposed development for Riverside South site, New York City

Street. Despite elaborate artist's impressions. Trump's office is reticent about the scheme's architects. Apparently Philip Johnson had a hand in it somewhere but, it would seem, most of the buildings have yet to be designed; ideas on a postcard to Trump Tower. Stranger than the fact that Trump's organisation cannot name the architects of the huge row of towers fronting onto the Hudson River, would seem to be the fact that the New York City authorities are prepared to grant development rights without knowing the details of the proposed buildings. As ever was. For all that I have heard, Rockefeller was equally vague about his proposals until they popped out of the Manhattan mud.

As famous as Joan Collins, as infamous as the late Robert Maxwell, as extreme as JR Ewing, and a dollar billionaire, the author of the best-selling *The Art of the Deal* peaked around 1988 when he topped out his property portfolio with the acquisition of Manhattan's famed Plaza Hotel.

Just as our Lord (Peter) Palumbo, past Chair-man of the Arts Council and development baron of the City's Mansion House Square, built his fortune on that of his father, so Trump was handed a good start in life from his father, Fred, who made his millions collecting rents in Brooklyn and Queens.

Trump came to public attention not so much for his buildings, although Trump Tower was on the map, but for the shenanigans with his previous wife, Ivana, who took him to the cleaners and settled up so that Donald could start again with model Marla Maples, much to the delight of *Hello* Magazine for which he must provide endless copy or at least the chance of a picture or two.

So now that all these family problems are apparently behind him and he seems to know more than a little of his pluralist mind about architecture, where is the Trump property-based empire going? How will he spend his millions on architectural patronage? Does architecture feature at all in the way in which he sees his prop-erty empire? Or is it just buildings with bits on?

'What sort of characteristics do you look for when making that very important decision, buying real estate, when you have to decide who's going to design the building?'

'It's very, very difficult. I like to get somebody with a big reputation because I think the reputa-tion pays for itself. I like to get somebody who also is known for giving good working drawings. That's something that you don't write about as much but a very big part of architecture is getting the drawings in such a form that you can build those drawings out. And a lot of great architects don't know the first thing about working drawings. They're good with a brush,

but they're not good with a pencil.'

'When you were younger and planning your way, did you know any architects by name?'

'I've always admired the great architects: Frank Lloyd Wright, Philip Johnson who works for me now and is doing some jobs for me.'

'What's he doing?'

'He's doing a development on the west side of Manhattan'

'Why did you choose Johnson?'

'I chose Johnson on the west side on my River-side South project because I just think he is a really great architect. He's proven to be an enduring talent and a great architect.'

There is a whole heap of Trump patronage on which to feast a critical eye: Trump Tower, Riverside South, Trump Parc, Trump Palace, Trump Plaza and wait for it, Trump Taj Mahal Casino Resort. If this is patronage of quality architecture even in line with Trump Tower, then I'm off to Agra. Chen Sam puts it like this: 'the Taj Mahal became the first casino in Atlantic City gaming history to break the $400 million gross revenue mark.' Well it may have done that. Which presumably in gaming circles is a real challenge. But as architecture it's about as valuable as the Taj Mahal Tandoori and Take-away in Neasden High Street.

How can the man that commissioned and seriously built a not half bad tower in Fifth Avenue (setting the atrium aside as a temporary aberration) wake up one morning and commis-sion a casino in Atlantic City designed to look like the Taj Mahal? What does he think about the proper path of the development of architecture today? 'Well, you're just not going with the trend. I don't think the trend is going to be as it was before. You'll have glass boxes, great glass buildings, you'll have old fashioned buildings, you'll have perhaps the AT&T types and right next to it the Seagram types.'

Donald Trump remains one of the world's most important individual architectural patrons. How is he going to spend his billions of dollars over the next six years? How will he decided how to spend them? Who's responsibility is it to deter-mine how he spends them? One thing is for sure, Trump will make an amazing and lasting mark on the architectural face of America as long as he has the courage to make decisions. And I guess that with Marla under his wings he will do that as long as he has breath.

But how will he choose between Philip Johnson or the architect that designed the Taj

FROM ABOVE: Trump Palace, New York City, 1991; Trump Parc, New York City, 1988; Trump Plaza, New York City, 1984

Mahal, not the real one, but the one where coins fill slots and balls rattle round roulette wheels?

The responsibility lies not on his shoulders but on that of the American architectural profession. If Trump is going to spend his millions and billions and zillions on buildings worth a penny piece, he needs the power of influence on his decision making. Philip Johnson will have evaporated into the ether long before most of Trump's ideas have come to fruition. Stern is old and, I guess, tired.

I ended our forty minute Manhattan conversation by asking him which young architects he knew – 'I know them, I haven't been as involved with them as I have been the old guard, well known famous, accomplished architects. And perhaps I should be, but I'm almost unwilling to take the chance.'

'Why?'

'I'm building $200 million buildings and I don't wanna hire somebody that maybe turns out not to be good. There is a reason for somebody's reputation usually.'

'So you prefer an older, mature architect?'

'I prefer somebody that's proven something because the buildings that I build are so big, so important and so expensive that I'm really not willing to take the chance as of this moment. But I may be.'

It seems to me that the challenge is to persuade Trump and his ilk to understand why architecture of quality can add value to value, change one location into another and build personal monuments which enhance the personality and ego of the purposeful patron.

Donald Trump is only 47 so there is plenty of time to give him the information he needs to scatter his mind with ideas. His door is open. It may take some time to get through, but every architect with an idea worth its real estate value should give Trump a chance to spend his money where it counts and make it count.

My hour scheduled in big D's diary was more than a little disappointing. A late start and a long interruption for that all important call to China cut our conversation down to size. My photographer told me this was par for the course in New York and that Trump was no worse than most of his ilk when it came to the niceties: after all I had only travelled half way around the world for our conversation: but I suppose I shouldn't have expected more from a man with such a conspicuous tabloid reputation. But most disappointing of all, he turned out to be exactly as I had expected. There was nothing more or less to him than I had been led to believe. If only he had had an enthusiasm for the paintings of Jackson Pollock or even a healthy addiction to Gershwin, but it turns out that the man who commissioned an Atlantic City casino to look like the Taj Mahal relaxes to 'one of the greatest talents there is . . . Elton John.'

FROM ABOVE: Trump Taj Mahal, Atlantic City, New Jersey, 1990; two views of Trump Castle, Atlantic City, New Jersey, 1985

DYNAMICAL SYMMETRIES

MATHEMATICAL SYNTHESIS BETWEEN CHAOS THEORY (COMPLEXITY), FRACTAL GEOMETRY AND THE GOLDEN MEAN
Nigel Reading

Morphology is not only a study of material things and of the forms of material things, but has its dynamical aspect ... in terms of force, of the operations of energy. This is a great theme. Boltzmann, writing in 1886 on the second law of thermodynamics, declared that available energy was the main object at stake in the struggle for existence and the evolution of the world.

D'Arcy Thompson, *On Growth and Form*, 1942

Boltzmann is known to us as the first to provide a probabilistic, statistical interpretation of entropy. This is simply the tendency of everything to cool to a minimum energy or temperature – known as thermal equilibrium. The route to this second law of thermodynamics is via increasing disorder.

The great paradox of the second law is the evident, complex hierarchical order we see all about us. How is this structured information (expressed in constantly oscillating patterns of matter and energy) allowed to coalesce from this tendency towards the random – towards increasing entropy?

Dynamical systems theory also deals with probability and can therefore allow us to synthesise thermodynamics and so-called Chaos. The really interesting area here though, is the transition zone between ordered, stable systems at equilibrium (high entropy) and disordered and unstable Chaotic (low entropy) ones. This is known as the region of alternatively, Complexity, Emergence, Edge of or Anti-Chaos. (Nascent science debates nomenclature habitually.)

This transition zone is occupied mathematically, by The Golden Mean. This ratio acts as an optimised probability operator, like a binary switch, whenever we observe the progressive evolution of a dynamical system. In this review, we shall cover some demonstrations of this behaviour.

As far as architectural application is concerned, we must look at the temporal as well as the spatial, at how quite literally, the dynamics (of systems applications) can inform the statics (forms) of building. The aesthetics of the banal imitation of some motif of fractal geometry is simply missing half the picture! Aristotle implied that the proper investigation required was one of **telos**, of form being the result of the process that engendered it.

All fractal forms are self-similar scaled copies of an original, Chaotic systems also always possess this fractal quality. To produce these forms, a recursive feedback regime must be operating. Feedback (encoding similarities) underlies the entire subject, and is the basis of the thesis research (undertaken at

the Engineering and Science Faculty, University of Westminster) that underlies this review.

This research began several years ago as an intuition that The Golden Mean, or *Phi* for short, (as a self-similar scaling series) must have been fractal in nature. By extension, it seemed plausible that *Phi* may also have been embedded in higher dimensional, dynamical systems as an attractor of some kind.

The major clue leading to the above interpretations can be seen in the fact that *Phi* is simultaneously both an arithmetic and quadratic expansion of the simplest possible kind. This immediately places it in both the **linear** and **non-linear** realms, and as an effective bridge, operating between the two.

Virtually every aspect of fractal geometry and type of dynamical system can be expressed by variations upon the simple quadratic iterator: $X = X^2 + c$ which expresses the particular type of feedback being examined, *Phi* can be expressed by a related but more archetypal variation to derive the Fibonacci series: $X_{n-1} = X_n + X_{n-1}$ which incrementally gravitates towards a particular ratio which possesses unique qualities. Numerically, it can be derived from the relation $(1+\sqrt{5})/2$. For example, if one divides *Phi* by its reciprocal you derive its square: $\emptyset/(1/\emptyset) = \emptyset^2$. Additionally, *Phi* is the unique ratio that fulfils: $1/\emptyset + 1/\emptyset^2 = 1$ in other words, *Phi* is the only possible quadratic partitioning of One. This leads us to the other cardinal feature of *Phi*. There is only one proportional division of One possible using two terms, with the third being One itself. From Euclid's ELEMENTS Book Five, Theorem Three: 'A straight line is said to have been cut in extreme and mean ratio when, as the whole line is to the greater segment, so is the greater to the less.'

As we shall see, this reciprocal, squaring behaviour about One, or Unity, as it is more properly termed, is far from being mathematically trivial. All feedback loops deterministically involve the passage of time. The quadratic iterator is derived from Newton's calculus, and from a period when Nature was seen as a mechanistic and reversible automaton. Recent science demonstrates that in fact it consists of both the above and irreversible processes, known as the entropy barrier or the arrow of time. The Golden Mean can also be seen as mathematically (because of the above) the simplest and most stable way of communing or mediating between the two, as we shall see.

As mentioned, iterated recursive loops must occur over a certain time interval and have a beginning and an end. This is analogous (derived from the Greek for proportional action) to the initiation of a system at the apex of a cone, and a progressive winding around its extruding surface (with cone length being the age of

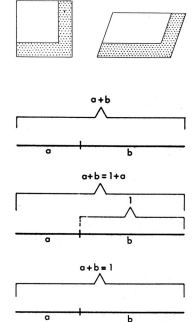

$$\Phi = 1 + \cfrac{1}{1 + \cfrac{1}{1 + \cfrac{1}{1 + \cfrac{1}{1 + \cfrac{1}{1 + \cdots}}}}}$$

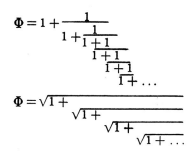

$$\Phi = \sqrt{1 + \sqrt{1 + \sqrt{1 + \sqrt{1 + \cdots}}}}$$

FROM ABOVE: Fractal figures; the line constitutes a wholeness, a unity; first case – the whole is more than one; second case – the whole is equal to one; arithmetic and quadratic expansion

the system). The resulting two dimensional spiral inscribed on the cone surface represents an extruded origin, being One, constantly growing over time but never changing its shape, an example of its optimum stability. The world line of this system heads from the apex to the origin of the disk-base and is irreversible. However, there is mathematically, the reciprocal case: another world line heading in the opposite direction, at all times, producing together, a spindle form, with an infinitely thin pinch-point joining them. This can be seen explicitly in the complex plane, as we shall see. This is how *Phi* mediates between the finite and infinite attractors, and allows for infinite co-dimensionally and reversible/irreversible processes in its action.

The feedback loop which describes *Phi* is an arithmetic **linear** operator, (like a binary switch: 0 or 1, off or on) representing the winding or rotation number of the inscribed spiral, which is conventionally represented as a multiple of 2π. This is superposed with its expansion ratio; 1 : 1.618 ... which is quadratic (logarithmic) and therefore **non-linear**. The former is reversible (and finite) while the latter is not (and infinite – being numerically irrational).

This binary switching process, unique to *Phi*, known also as an Eigen, rescaling or renormalisation operator, is analogous to the tossing of a coin, a chance or stochastic process, that allows a probabilistic interpretation. This mathematics is also the paradigm for quantum mechanics, dynamical systems, and the relativistic (with appropriate super--positions) or in other words, the maths of chance and arbitrarily large numbers. The *Phi* operator has been shown by physicists to be a super-stable mechanism (most resistant to perturbation) by which systems can evolve increasing complexity of information structure over time. This stability is due to its optimising of a geometric scaling of itself and confirms *Phi* as imbedded within non-linear dynamical systems.

So *Phi* is a paragon of **telos**, it is an image of its own self-generative process translated in scale, over time. It is a recursive feedback loop acting as a rudimentary self-replicating memory machine that has a manifestation in the linear and non-linear, at all scales, and in any dimension. We can confirm these assertions by first noting *Phi*'s fractal dimension. This measure of the complexity of the *Phi* spiral produced a dimension of One, it being linear in nature and form. As mentioned, we can use the quadratic iterator to demonstrate not only the pervasive nature of *Phi*, but also its intrinsic relationship with dynamical systems. We already see that it is an archetypal feedback system that in turn generates a protofractal that is nevertheless, linear (one dimensional). This is uniquely paradoxical because to be fractal a form must be of non-integral dimension, between dimensions, in fact.

The one-step feedback loop derived from the iterator: $X = X^2 + c$ (the equation for a circle – a section of the *Phi* temporal evolution cone) with c = -1, produces what is known as the **super-attractive case**. Here two fixed values rather than the normal one are produced, being: 0 and -1. In the case of any other c-value the iterations of feeding the product back into the equation rapidly produce what is a hallmark of Chaos; sensitive dependence on initial

conditions – or exponential error propagation!

Remarkably, even if we alter values for Xo we still derive the same results. This makes the cycle as resistant to perturbation as is possible; O and -1 represent the repelling fixed points for the equation which in turn, generate a super-attractive orbit, between them. The orbit itself is strictly periodic but of the lowest dynamic period possible (being two) and therefore crucially, consumes **the least energy to maintain**. This is why *Phi*'s deterministic switching action under infinite iteration, must also have, following Boltzmann, a thermodynamic interpretation; (after Roger Penrose) where: **entropy = k log V** (with Boltzmann's constant (k) as Unity and the volume of the phase space (V) as increasing, arithmetically and quadratically).

The constant c = -1 will rapidly produce error if even infinitesimally deviated from, and so represents an island of perfect stability surrounded by a seething maelstrom of Chaos. Solving the paired equations for the system (known as a two-step loop) produced $\emptyset = (1 + \sqrt{5})/2$, the Golden Mean. It is confirmed as the mathematical entity on the very cusp of Chaos. This is, considering its super-stability and attractive nature, a remarkable result – which has been confirmed by several mathematicians and physicists in numerous and diverse fields of inquiry. (See bibliography).

This point is of the highest mathematical significance for renovating our understanding of *Phi* in terms of **dynamical** systems and the immanent symmetry breaking action of thermodynamics, from which they are derived.

The Cantor Set is simply the equal division of a line into three parts, with the middle third being removed, scaling down to **infinitely** many intervals of **finite** length. It is the three term division of One, as opposed to the two term division of One by *Phi*. It underlies all Chaotic dynamics, in concert with *Phi*'s switching action. This is because it has both a binary and ternary expansion – and because it, too, communes between finite and infinite attractors.

Chaotic systems behave in a kneading fashion, mixing-in infinite permutations: known as ergodic behaviour. This can be again represented by a $\emptyset$ binary operator. When we examine the Feigenbaum diagram of systems period-doubling into Chaos we find not only the Golden Mean to be a paradigm for all the bifurcations in it – but also, that at the edge of Chaos, known as the Feigenbaum Point, the *Phi* operator produces an infinite Cantor Set, with *Phi* proportions. The initial operations are illustrated. This is a mathematical **singularity**.

Bands of order in the Feigenbaum diagram occur at a fixed scaling ratio, and correspond exactly to super-attractive periodic fixed points like those mentioned above. The bifurcations again, contain *Phi*. In fact, all the various universal constants found within the Feigenbaum diagram are derived from the Golden Mean's deterministic rescaling operation. This is how *Phi* is imbedded within dynamical systems, as the **universal binary shift operator**, or primary Eigenfunction. All constants so derived are Eigenvalues of this operator.

The Rössler strange attractor (essentially an

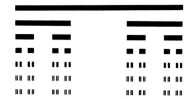

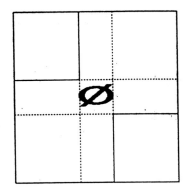

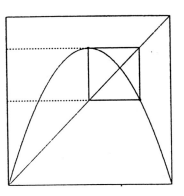

FROM ABOVE: Cantor set – finite and the infinite; two examples of the Cantor set from Feigenbaum diagram with Ø proportions

archetypal picture of a Chaotic system in four dimensional phase-space) is used to model autocatalytic sets such as the famous BZ reactions seen at the Architectural Association's recent Complexity conference. Note the *Phi* spirals in the cellular automaton model. The attractor is a Cantor Set in 4D, over time – and is a means of representing *Phi* in phase-space at the Feigenbaum Point, on the edge of Chaos.

The Complex plane can be likened to the mapping of a sphere onto a plane and is the result of the Riemannian geometry used to model quantum and relativistic behaviour. A dimension shift is implicit here, as an equilateral triangle inscribed on the sphere will have 270° as the sum of its angles: 60° becomes 90°, an effective dimension shift of 1.5 (which is the *Phi*/Cantor Set ratio: 1/(2/3)). To move from one spatial dimension to another requires this operation.

Complex numbers have a **real** and **imaginary** component, so as to express planar coordinates. If we place two basins of attraction (imagine a pendulum and two magnets) in this plane we can perhaps simulate the behaviour of *Phi* at either the quantum or relativistic scales. We know the Golden Mean acts as a super-attractive orbit between two repelling fixed points, so if we again run the equation for the circle, with c = -1 , we produce a Julia Set, (after its originator), for the Golden Mean.

The Mandelbrot Set is the encyclopedia of all Julia Sets, and explicitly confirms *Phi* as of critical significance in its morphology. Again, with c = 1 we see *Phi* as the locus of the Period Two disk of the Mandelbrot Set.

Geometrically, we are looking at sets with two basins of attraction: the infinite escape set, and the finite prisoner set. Their boundaries are not only infinite, and infinitely varied – but also contain self-similar, slightly mutated copies of themselves. The P2 Disk itself, acts as a geometric oscillator.

If we look closely at the *Phi* Julia Set, we can measure 1: 1/Ø² in its proportions; exactly *Phi*'s reciprocal, quadratic action. The Complex plane itself can be mapped by a system analogous to electrical force equipotentials and field lines. When we describe the *Phi* Julia Set fixed point behaviour, we see two field lines landing on the pinch-point (as with the spindle example) for 1/Ø, representing an angle doubling from 1/3 to 2/3 of 2π. Now, **angle doubling** in the Complex plane is equivalent to squaring in the Euclidean plane, and to an oscillation of the binary shift operator.[1] This action should confirm *Phi*'s behaviour as an operator in the quantum and relativistic dimensions (note that space-time itself is fractal, in between dimensions). Because the fixed points are on the boundary of the Julia Set, we see explicitly, that *Phi* exists on the boundary between the finite prisoner and infinite escape sets, on the **edge of Chaos**, in fact. The Golden Mean is also intrinsically dynamic, its action is one of perpetual reciprocal oscillation, exactly and uniquely replicating the dynamics of the unit circle. The *Phi* Julia Set, centred at the origin of Period Two dynamics, is the only set that acts so.

This again, allows *Phi* to operate at all scales and dimensions, and confirms it as when infinitely iterated, the mathematically most stable attractive orbit for achieving a singularity. The fixed points themselves

confirm the orbit between the finite (0) and infinite (-1) attractors.

The squaring of the circle therefore, has an expression in the Complex plane, which confirms the Golden Mean's profound dynamical and symmetric action.

If we then compare the Mandelbrot Set with the Feigenbaum Diagram we can see how the Period One Cardoid of the former corresponds exactly with the single, equilibrium trajectory of the latter. The Period Two Disk with *Phi* as its super-attractive centre, exactly matches the first bifurcation - confirming *Phi*, geometrically as the paradigm for stochastic bifurcation. All the subsequent bands of order in the latter (which occur at a fixed scaling ratio derived from *Phi*) precisely match the micro Mandelbrot Sets along the horizontal axis of the Set.

This geometric evidence confirms *Phi* as the optimum oscillating mechanism that mediates between ordered, equilibrium systems and disordered, nonequilibrium ones. It allows an oscillating orbit to access the infinitely fecund morphologies of Chaos, recapitulate them back into its super-stable orbit: and therefore permit system growth and morphogenesis. **It is the paradigm for systems evolution**. The Golden Mean therefore represents absolute **order**, as an orbit, but when deviated from, and/or under iteration over time, also allows for stochastic **Chaos**. Since the passage from one to the other is governed by the second law of thermodynamics, responsible for irreversible processes, this also makes *Phi* the optimum operator for both linear reversibility and non-linear irreversibility.

Various cellular automata simulations also confirm *Phi*'s structure-enhancing evolutionary action, to the point of researchers citing it as an inevitable target for natural selection. The same can be said for various investigations into plasma and quantum-scattering physics, pure maths of dynamical systems and fractal dimension, and ecosystem simulations – to name a few. All cite *Phi* as an invariant attractor behaving in some or all of the ways discussed above. (Please consult the bibliography references.)

A most interesting study by the Danish-born physicist Per Bak models behaviour known as Self-Organised Criticality: in these models he observes reciprocal squaring behaviour which is still considered a mysterious power law. This law is observed in the oscillating behaviour of the sun, light pulses from other galaxies or the intermittent flow of current through a resistor, or of water through a channel. The behaviour is also self-similar at all scales, as it gravitates towards **edge of Chaos** criticality, and so it seems reasonable to intuit it to be another manifestation of Golden Mean dynamical behaviour.

Chris Langton of the Santa Fé Institute, dedicated exclusively to Complexity research, likens order to a solid, disorder to a gas, and believes a liquid form of Complexity occupies a phase transition region between the two. The Institute is essentially exploring this **edge of Chaos** region by means of various computer simulations, looking for a putative new second law of thermodynamics. Considering the evidence above, it is likely that the Golden Mean will form a significant part of this exploration.

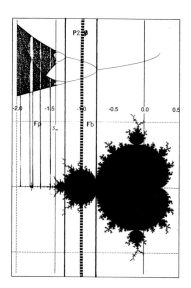

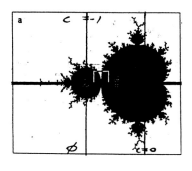

FROM ABOVE: BZ reaction and Ø spirals; Mandelbrot Set Feigenbaum diagram synthesis; Ø-Mandelbrot Set synthesis

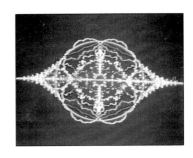

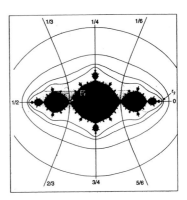

It seems clear now that the Golden Mean can certainly be reconciled with the new science, which reveals a profound **dynamical** aspect to its action. Without prolonging this review excessively, here are some brief examples of how the assimilation of dynamical systems knowledge, married with new engineering, materials and systems technology, might reinvent the statics of architecture:

Climate control will increasingly become a hybrid between active elements, such as mechanical ventilation, and the passive, such as natural ventilation. Low-tech, vernacular ideas for climate control, such as the atrium, fused with the higher technology of computerised solar gain louvres with integrated photoelectrics, for example, are already in use. The future is green building. Stack-effect, evaporative cooling, cross ventilation and even aerodynamics are some of the hybrid strategies currently in use. (Note here that the Lorenz attractor, related to the Rössler attractor, is a model of thermal convection flows – and therefore directly applicable to passive climate control design on a micro-climatic scale.) All are systems (or functions) leading form.

A facade incorporating electrochromic glass that is linked into a central processing unit with a parallel-processing neural network can instantaneously regulate solar gain by adjusting facade opaqueness, depending on the facade's orientation. That network can also minimise overall building energy load by only lighting, ventilating, heating or cooling occupied spaces. Such systems may display a form of metabolic homeostasis known in artificial intelligence circles as Emergence, allowing for simple system memory and learning capacities. This has everything to do with recursive feedback loops being employed in environmental services design. Dynamics can synthesise clearly, with statics.

Polyvalent facades will, using liquid crystal technologies (glass is made from silica – as is the LCD and the silicon chip) convey graphic information on the skins of buildings for the external world to observe. Chameleon buildings will for example, be able to react to passing clouds, altering facade U-values and values for solar gain, to compensate for those clouds, or the tracking shadows cast by neighbouring buildings. The pixel-like elements of a facade might communicate ambiently in the manner of some cellular automata, feeding back continually with environmental stimuli. A similar ambient music real-time soundscape might therefore truly 'melt' the 'Frozen Music' of architecture: defining it as a musical instrument itself, as played by its environment.

A major design constraint (and therefore, opportunity) of passive climate control is that strategies and final design solutions must adapt to the cultures and local climates of sites: hence the earlier use of the term 'Vernacular', as a **methodology**, not an aesthetic, of Complexity.

This is not an appeal to imitation but rather a recognition that just as in the past, differing climates and cultures will deterministically produce different design solutions, and produce discrete architecture appropriate to their climatic and cultural environment. This produces a distinct and profound **identity** and variety for architectural form throughout the World.

The Modern Movement's main failure was that it became a metaphor for the Newtonian mechanistic paradigm. It imposed an anonymous homogeneity worldwide (the International Style is also the most internationally loathed). It ignored the vernacular architectural diversity of cultural response; to a plethora of environmental constraints – identity was forbidden for the Machine Age. **How then do we transcend this failure – and restore Identification?** What an investigation of the dynamics of the Golden Mean tells us, is that it is an optimum mathematical paragon of **energy-efficiency**: this is achieved as an ultimate means of generating information structures of energy and matter. Rather than merely imitating the statics of Eigenvalue proportions, we are now also liberated to epitomise the Mean through elegance of: structure (the bearing of dynamic forces), and the economies of **vernacular-informed green architecture**.

Chaos shows how appropriate it is to term our age, the Information Age: one which increasingly exists to exchange and enhance pure information, just as the Irreversibility – driven evolution imperative of the Universe and of Life itself demonstrates. Architecture, as a cultural artefact that inevitably will be imbued with the current zeitgeist, should assimilate as much of the implications of *Phi*/Chaos dynamical symmetry; as its procurers and practitioners will allow.

Suffice to say, Complexity is found at the edge of Chaos, which is epitomised by the Golden Mean: therefore its representation is creation itself.

Reference: 1 Angle doubling is also the squaring of the modulus for the 'collapse of the wave-function' measurement problem, for the Schrödinger equation in Quantum mechanics. This is where the equation switches probabilistically from the linearity of reversibility to the non-linearity of irreversibility.

Bibliography: *Chaos and Fractals* (Fractals for the Classroom), Vols 1 and 2 Heinz-Otto Peitgen, Hartmut Jurgens, Dietmar Saupe, Springer-Verlag, New York 1992; *Order from Chaos*, Ilya Prigogine and Isabelle Stengers, Flamingo 1985; *Chaos*, James Gleick, (Cardinal 1988) Abacus; *The Structure of the Cosmos*, Constantinos Kalarmaras, 1992; *Number* by John McLeish, Flamingo 1992. *Searching for Certainty* by John L Casti, Abacus 1993; *The Elements of Dynamic Symmetry* by Jay Hambridge, reprinted from the 'Diagonal' C. 1919, 1920 by Yale University Press; *The Geometry of Art and Life* by Matila Ghyka, published by Dover 1977 after Sheed and Ward, New York 1946; *Architectural Space in Ancient Greece* by C. A. Doxiadis C Massachusetts Institute of Technology 1972, first published 1937; *Gödel, Escher, Bach: An Eternal Golden Braid* by Douglas R Hofstadter, Penguin 1980; *Fractals: Non-Integral Dimensions and Applications* edited by G Cherbit, John Wiley + Sons Ltd; *The Fractal Geometry of Nature* by Benoit B Mandelbrot, W H Freeman & Co, New York 1977; *Sacred Geometry, Philosophy and Practice*, Robert Lawler, Thames and Hudson, 1982; *On Growth and Form* by D'Arcy Thompson, Cambridge University Press 1961; *Complexity, The Emerging Science at the Edge of Order and Chaos* by Mitchell Waldrop, Penguin 1992; *Iterated Maps on the Interval as Dynamical Systems* by Pierre Collet and Jean-Pierre Eckmann, Phi, Progress in Physics, Birkhauser, Boston, 1980; *Order in Chaos* edited by D. Campbell and H. Rose, Physica 7D, North-Holland, Amsterdam, 1983.

FROM ABOVE: Ø-Golden Mean Julia Set; Phi-Julia Set; Ø-Fixed Point Angle Doubling: Reciprocal Squaring Behaviour

AND HERE'S ONE I DESIGNED EARLIER

The self build market is expected to represent 25 percent of domestic housing stock in the next decade. Statistics based on government VAT returns for part of the total, indicate that the market is worth £650m per annum (£65,000 per house for 10,000 houses). About half as many again are outside the VAT statistics making a total of 15,000 new owner built homes which is more than those constructed by any two of the major national developers together. Conversely, although there have been signs of recovery recently, architectural employment overall has declined since the late 80s as architects find themselves in something of a self-imposed exile in design as a result of delegating technical and menial roles in order to 'legitimise' the profession. Can architects afford to ignore growing areas of the industry such as self build? Or, from a more positive angle, should they not leap at the chance to mould the shape of the housing of tomorrow?

The market was opened up by speculative developers who offered off-the-peg houses. The recent move to consumer choice was a result of the recession in the speculative sector which meant that in less than a decade the housing market changed from being a seller's to a buyer's market. The self build market, is driven by two factors: that the families concerned want to have new homes that are uniquely their own, and that the cost savings are often in excess of a year's family income. This often leads to the assumption that self builders are led by the profit motive, but evidence shows that profit is secondary to wanting to get their own home built exactly as they want.

Most new detached homes in Europe are commissioned by their purchasers. In France the figure is over 50 percent, in Germany and Italy over 60 percent, while in Austria 85 percent of all new home are built for families who started by buying their own land, although the percentage of owner occupiers in most countries is lower than in the UK. In America it is 30 percent and only in Japan is the figure below ours because most housing stock is built through a corporation.

Murray Armor author of *Building Your Own Home*, claims that 'it is surely inevitable that we shall follow the rest of the world and that within a decade our medium and low density homes will

be built to order as a matter of course'.

Only six percent of self build homes in Britain use the services of an architect. European restrictions on planning permission are such that proposals will only be accepted under the stamp of an architect. In Britain, while it is a criminal offence to use the title 'architect' if not registered with ARCUK (Architects Regulation Council of the United Kingdom), it is perfectly possible for a proposal to be granted planning permission without the said 'stamp'. The adoption of European standards as we develop closer ties with the European Community must work in the profession's favour. However, it has been suggested that while this is 'something to contemplate', proper representation and a higher profile might create more incentive for people to use architects rather than having to make it a legal requirement.

How exactly can architects capitalise on the growing self build market? Amy Charmier, Market Research Officer at the RIBA, claims that architects seeking to become involved would have to become acquainted with current demographic trends such as the overall decrease in employment and the increase in longevity.

There are several areas in which architects could play an important role. From a purely creative angle, the architectural input could range from 'kit/mail order designs' where catalogue companies commission a design (such as the French designer, Philippe Starck's 'La maison de Starck' advertised through the Parisian Trois Suisse catalogue at £95 to £120 thousand), to enabling community builders to express themselves through design.

Kit houses are not a new thing, indeed, at one end of the scale nomadic tents are a form of kit house while at the other, even Nicholas Grimshaw's Seville Expo Pavilion was designed to be able to be dismantled and reconstructed elsewhere. But taking this century in isolation, the RIBA supplied pattern books until the late 1940s. After the war pre-fab led to the mass supply of custom-made parts to speed up the process of reconstruction. In the 60s, variations on the self build idea included solutions such as the portacabin, the mobile home, Richard Rogers' 'Zip-up House', Archigram's Plug-in capsules, and more recently Richard Horden's 'Yacht House 1' etc. Walter Segal interpreted

FROM ABOVE: The ubiquitous 'neo-tudor' dream-house; Architype's Lewisham based Co-operative – a good example of the specific tailor made designs achieved through discussions with a self build group; Diggers Co-operative Houses Brighton – Architype's design is based on the Walter Segal house type

this theme in a community conscious vein and his example precipitated the formation of organisations such as his namesake, the Walter Segal Self Build Trust and the Association of Self build Architects.

In 1986, *Architectural Design* staged an international competition for 'A House for Today' sponsored by Barratt Developments PLC. Several fundamental points concerning self build were raised: Robert Krier pointed out that you don't get urban space if you build detached houses in their own gardens and Terry Farrell emphasised the need for integral flexibility to allow expansion and self expression. Starck acknowledges this last point in his design which encourages reinterpretation of flexible elements so that he does not 'make the buyer an architectural victim, living in a Starck house with Starck furniture'.

From a 'community minded' perspective, self build housing provides low income clients with the opportunity to reap financial benefit from their own efforts –'sweat equity'. It also provides training in the building trade on an apprenticeship level. Jonathan Hines of the Architype Design Co-operative believes that working with people sparks off greater creativity since 'there are more ideas going in' than designing in isolation 'where the designer *thinks* they know what people want' which often leads to a standard solution.

This goes to show that design features at both ends of the self build market – it is not always 'dictated' by the self builder but it can be 'directed' by the architect. By helping community builders to provide good quality, tailor made architecture, architects could put a stop to the ubiquitous ticky tacky boxes typical of speculative developments of the 60s and 70s and to the monotonous neo-Tudor of the 80s.

Increased involvement with the self build market might also serve to reintroduce the creative and technical sides of the profession. It might even precipitate the development of the 'architect-builder'. By re-identifying with the holistic perception of the image of an 'architect', such trained professionals could lend their knowledge of technical innovation to streamline the design process.

Many of these avenues have been explored. Historically, apart from the perceived lack of creativity, architects have not become involved in the self build market because while the fee system is set the hours are not. Cost certainty is obviously a prerequisite of self build schemes so the question of professional involvement in this growing market must be approached laterally. Working from the premise that only six percent of self built homes use an architect and that one of their main objectives is self expres-

sion, surely one way of resolving this would involve introducing architects to facilitate this desire.

The main issue is firstly that time is money and secondly that design is considered to be a dispensable element in realising construction. With the advance in computer technology, the time/design ratio can also be capitalised on by the layperson. New, 'Fast CAD Systems' enable laypersons to design their home inside and out providing them with information and advice that might previously have been sought through an architect. The race is on – if the time element could be decreased the design element would become more affordable. While some believe that 'La maison de Starck' is a gimmick, it might provide the key. The Trois Suisse package includes, among other things, a video of the stages of construction, a full set of detailed plans and product requirements. As with other product designs, the designer/architect takes the risk on development costs by selling his initial idea for a modest amount but is paid on a royalties basis for any subsequent sales. This would avoid the imbalance between time consumed and fee paid that can become a problem with self build. The public appeal, cost, flexibility and quality of the 'kit' would be self regulating avoiding the (perceived?) problem of making the client a victim of the architect's solution.

The main difficulty for architects entering this commercial arena is that traditionally they have been trained in the scenario of a direct relationship with the client in order to tailor the building to suit their needs. Resolving the conflict between 'tailor made' and 'speculative' would require commercial nous and flexible designs that allow self-expression. Philippe Starck claims that his house is the 'house everyone has dreamed of' and indeed the response to the overall design seems to have been very positive. However it is important to target the market's purchasing power because while everyone can dream, many people would not be able to afford the secluded site required for Starck's glass walled house.

'Time is money' is the catchphrase of this latter half of the 20th century. Surely it is about time we started making the ratio work in our favour. According to a recent report two other world class architects Aldo Rossi and Frank Gehry have been asked to provide mail-order homes for Les Trois Suisse. Gehry's office denies any knowledge of this saying that 'it is not something Gehry would be interested in'. Traditionally the response might have been 'he can afford not to be' but if we can alter the equation between time and money, using professional architectural knowledge to prevent a consequent drop in standards then perhaps mail-order homes will be in everyone's interest.

Katherine MacInnes

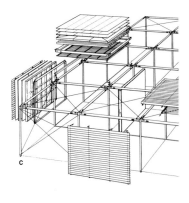

FROM ABOVE: Philippe Starck's La maison de Starck; *the kit for* La maison de Starck:' *handbook, illustrated by Starck, video of the construction stages and plans giving estimates for the materials required. Cost £585; Richard Horden, detail of the diagram of* Yacht House 1, *1983: 'The skin can be solid, open, louvred, trellised or incorporate open lights or blinds. Cost £55,000'*

BANK OF LUXEMBOURG HEADQUARTERS
ARQUITECTONICA

The Bank of Luxembourg aimed to make its new headquarters building a major component of its communication strategy. In an effort to be global, the Bank asked Arquitectonica to design the building. The furniture and graphics are the work of Jean Michael Wilmotte; the lighting was designed by the plastics technicians and lighting engineers of L'Observatoire; the gardens are the work of Jacques WIRTZ and Fiorenzo Cavallini took responsibility for the execution of the project.

The site is located at the focal point of the Luxembourg financial district. The building is developed within a tight envelope defined by zoning regulations. There are three elements to the composition.

A rectangular volume, clad in native beige stone, cantilevers forward to align with the sidewalk and the rest of the buildings along the boulevard. It has repetitive square windows with amber glass to match the stone tonality.

The orthogonal stone volume is seen as the contextual component in its relationship to the surrounding urban condition. In contrast, a glass tower is introduced as an object. It sits on axis with the vista at the end of the boulevard. The volume is curved and slants to engage the boulevard axis. Its transparency contrasts with the older stone buildings, but relates to the cadre of post-war office buildings in the city. The building is designed as a synthesis of the surroundings.

The two volumes described above are brought together by a parallelogram volume clad in polished black granite, emphasising their profile. The composition is anchored by a solid grey granite block placed at the corner, balancing the composition. At the base of the glass tower there is a large plaza terracing down to create a performance space. Behind, a small formal park links the new building with a dining and conference pavilion.

The image of the bank as a solid yet progressive institution is embodied in the architectural vocabulary. Throughout the building the use of the square, a stable form, contrasts with the ellipse, a dynamic form.

Photographs: Robin Barton

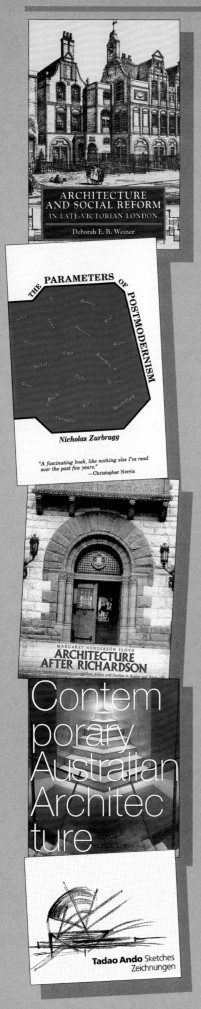

ARCHITECTURE AND SOCIAL RE-FORM In Late-Victorian London by Deborah E B Weiner, Manchester University Press, 244pp, b/w ills, HB £40

Many institutes of reform and philanthropy emerged in late Victorian London. They were intended to bring the redemptive values of English middle-class culture to the working-classes. Amidst the sea of squalid brick tenements and working-class two-up, two-down houses of late nineteenth-century London, new building types arose, large in scale and bold in their message: the triple-storeyed Queen Anne board schools, the mock Elizabethan settlement houses, an Arts and Crafts free public art gallery replete with mystic symbolism, and as first conceived, a new-Byzantine pleasure palace for the working classes. Weiner explains the social relations which informed the production and use of these buildings, analysing the relationship between the intentions of the founders and the architectural expression of their buildings, which drew upon contemporary myths of a peaceful and harmonious past.

THE PARAMETERS OF POST-MODERNISM by Nicholas Zurbrugg, Routledge, 180pp, PB, Price N/A

Nicholas Zurbrugg demonstrates how contemporary artistic creativity discredits popular apocalyptic theories. Based on his extensive interviews with a number of leading postmodern artists, writers and performers (Anderson, Baudrillard, Beckett, Cage, Glass, Rainer and Wilson for example) this book offers a challenging, positive view of postmodern culture.

Zurbrugg names the condition caused by the prevailing negative theories about postmodern culture the 'B-effect', a term derived from what he considers the fictions and contradictions in the work of a number of influential European writers and theorists (Brecht, Beckett, Barthes, Baudrillard, Bourdieu, and others) who have insisted on both the death of artistic innovation and the lack of a permanent reality. In the first section of *The Parameters of Postmodernism*, Zurbrugg considers the contradictions in the arguments of the B-effect writers and points to later writings in which they qualify their earlier, most infamous assertions.

In the second section of the book, Zurbrugg introduces the off-setting 'C-effect' of postmodern culture, an effect based on those more positive creative practices and theories best exemplified, he feels, by the work of American composer John Cage. Zurbrugg identifies additional aspects of the 'C-effect' in the multimedia experiments of other Americans, such as Anderson, Ashley, Glass, Monk, Rainer and Wilson, who interweave the new postmodern media with confidence and invention and those European artist and writers like Beuys, Carrington, Eco, Grass, Muller and Wolf who revive, modify and re-animate mythological, medieval, neoclassical, and folklore traditions. Zurbrugg argues that in each case – high-tech or revivalist – postmodern creativity culminates in highly positive syntheses of past, present, and futuristic materials.

ARCHITECTURE AFTER RICHARDSON Regionalism before Modernism – Longfellow, Alden and Harlow in Boston and Pittsburgh by Margaret Henderson Floyd, University of Chicago Press, 400 pages, b/w ills, HB £59

Most histories of American architecture after H H Richardson have emphasised the work of Louis Sullivan and Frank Lloyd Wright in the Middle West. By examining instead the legacy of three highly successful architects who were in practice simultaneously in New England and Western Pennsylvania from 1886 into the 1920s, Margaret Henderson Floyd underscores the architectural significance of another part of the nation. The careers, work and patronage of Alexander Wadsworth Longfellow Frank Ellis Alden and Alfred Branch Harlow are critically assessed. After Richardson's death the three set up their own practice.

Placing these architects in a broader context of American architectural and landscape history allows a strong cultural affinity between turn-of- the-century Boston and Pittsburgh to be revealed. Henderson Floyd also indicates an unsuspected link between the path of modernism from Richardson to Wright and the evolution of anti-modern imagery, manifested in regionalism.

CONTEMPORARY AUSTRALIAN ARCHITECTURE by Graham Jahn, Gordon and Breach Arts International, 250pp, colour ills, HB, Price N/A

Until quite recently, Australians have thought of themselves as a classless, commonsensical, anti-pretentious European people. Australian arts, architecture and culture generally have fed off a romanticised pioneering legend of the individual battling alone in a vast landscape. However, such perceptions of a homogeneous society and the bush myth have been giving way under the weight of great changes in Australian society. Immigration, multiculturalism and republicanism are only some of the significant forces that are now shaping substantially different Australian cultural values from those developed over the past 200 years since European colonisation. This book traces the fascinating development of new ideas in Australian architecture since 1975. Forty-five important buildings are documented. The selection incudes houses, offices, churches and sports stadia designed by Australian architects, or by Japanese or American architects working in Australia.

TADAO ANDO Sketches edited by Werner Blaser, preface by Mario Botta, Birkhäuser Verlag, 180pp, b/w ills, HB, Price N/A

In his introduction, Mario Botta claims that in investigating the work of Tadao Ando, one penetrates the aspirations, the hopes and expectations of a large part of our contemporary architectural culture. With great naturalness his architecture communicates the meaning and condition proper of 'place' and 'site' upon which the act of 'building' willed by man operates. It conveys the value, the significance and the message defined by a wall as it separates spaces; it also describes with great poetic power the intrinsic value of 'light' as a basic architectonic element – light reveals itself in all its cosmic depth, proffers itself as an instrument for measuring the passage of time. When it flow on a tangent along surfaces, that light which vibrates along cement walls, which takes its thickness from slightly wavy reliefs, is an indispensable instrument for this archi-

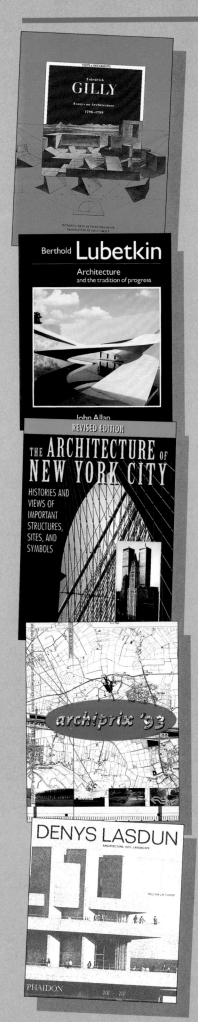

tecture so essential and rigorous. Botta considers that these three issues are central to an understanding of Ando's work.

FRIEDRICH GILLY Essays on Architecture 1796-99, introduced by Fritz Neumeyer, Getty Centre Publications and University of Chicago Press, 228pp, b/w ills, PB, Price N/A

When Friedrich Gilly died in 1800, at the age of 28, he had published only four short essays, and his executed works consisted of a few minor buildings still under construction. Nonetheless, by virtue of the influence that he – as a teacher colleague and friend – exerted on Berlin architects active during the first half of the 19th century, Gilly may justly be regarded as the founder of the Berlin architectural tradition. His legacy, moreover, extends into the 20th century.

The present volume seeks to afford new access to Friedrich Gilly's ideas on architecture by presenting for the first time annotated English translations of his four published essays and the unpublished descriptions of his proposed memorial to Frederick the Great. An introduction by Fritz Neumeyer clearly locates Gilly's work and ideas within their historical context and forcefully demonstrates the lasting influence that Gilly has had on architecture, particularly in Germany.

BERTHOLD LUBETKIN Architecture and the Tradition of Progress by John Allan, RIBA Publications, 628pp, b/w ills, HB, Price N/A

Berthold Lubetkin was a pivotal figure in the development of the Modern Movement in Britain. This pioneer architect was a survivor of the Russian Revolution, European traveller and intellectual, social commentator and, at the age of 81, RIBA Royal Gold Medallist. This publication combines drawings and photographs with extracts from Lubetkin's writings to provide an insight into this maverick personality. Lubetkin's belief in building design as an instrument of social progress was expressed in a determined pursuit of technical innovation underlaid by a profound appreciation of architecture's formal disciplines and emotive power. Lubetkin's chang-

ing attitude to Soviet developments is considered in conjunction with the other factors that in 1931 brought him to England where he founded the architectural practice, Tecton. Allan investigates the theoretical stance that set him apart from the architectural establishment and from his Modernist contemporaries.

THE ARCHITECTURE OF NEW YORK CITY Histories and Views of Important Structures, Sites and Symbols by Donald Martin Reynolds, John Wiley & Sons, Inc, 390pp, b/w ills, PB $29.95

The history of New York City is a rich pageant of culture, commerce, social change, and human drama stretching back 500 years. Dr Reynolds describes 90 of the city's most striking buildings, bridges, parks and places, informing the reader of why, when and how they were built, and by whom.

The history of the city's fabric is traced from its 16th-century Dutch canals and 18th-century farmhouses to the elevator buildings of the 1870s and the Art Deco, Bauhaus and Postmodern buildings. Some of the most idiosyncratic features exist on the 1913-30 Woolworth building; corbels feature the architect, Thomas R Johnston holding a model of the building and the client, Frank Woolworth paying for his building with nickels and dimes, since he paid for its construction with cash. Aspects of the city are examined with great warmth and optimism, for example the Manhattan skyline from the top of the Ferrybank Restaurant; Walt Whitman proclaimed that views such as this were 'the best, most effective medicine my soul has yet partaken'.

ARCHIPRIX '93 The best plans by Dutch students, Archiprix Foundation, 80pp, colour ills, PB fl 34.50

The Archiprix Foundation is a collaboration between seven higher educational institutions in the Netherlands in the fields of architecture, planning and landscape architecture. The Archiprix Foundation was set up in January 1992 and derives from the 'National FC Commission for Student Plans' established on the initiative of the 'Steering Committee for Experiments in Domestic Construction'.

Each year the institutions that teach design in the Netherlands select the best plans by their students for submission to Archipriz. The 21 plans submitted present a diverse state of affairs in Dutch design. Unlike most competitions, there is no common design task. Scale, issues, presentation, all of these differ with each plan. In her plan for the delta coast in Zeeland, Katrien Prak describes 'a land of space, thrashing waves and rock-solid dykes. Ever since the dams were erected the coast has been flooded with pleasure-seekers. They conquered the dams proclaiming them a free state for water sports enthusiasts. Her recreation 'scenario ' is characterised by an explosive development in recreation, using optimum accessibility and a dominant role for water sports.

DENYS LASDUN Architecture, City, Landscape by Willilam J R Curtis 239pp, Phaidon b/w ills, HB Price N/A

This study of the British architect, Denys Lasdun is based upon exhaustive study by Curtis of primary documentary sources and over 20 years of dialogue with the architect. It casts light on the meaning of such key works as the Bethnal Green housing clusters(1952-4), the Royal College of Physicians (1959), the University of East Anglia (1962) among others. Two chapters are devoted to the social history and design process of the National Theatre and Opera House (1965) which is currently the subject of much controversial debate. This book explores Lasdun's idea of architecture and 'urban landscape' in which buildings are thought of as 'hills and valleys' with towers, terraces and platforms forming the generic features. The book also investigates the ways in which Lasdun has extended the principles of the modern masters into new expressive territories, especially in the design of institutional buildings where he has absorbed, and transformed, influences as diverse as Frank Lloyd Wright, Le Corbusier, Mackintosh and Hawksmoor; but behind his work there is also a driving preoccupation with institutions, the city and 'nature'. Invaluable insights are afforded into British architectural history of the past 60 years.

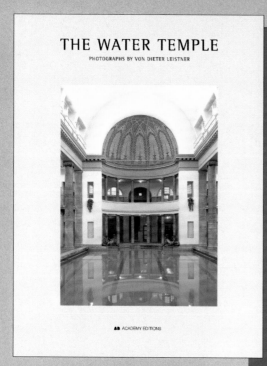

All the baths featured in this exqui-sitely illustrated volume were built between 1872-1940. Their architectural beauty and quality is revealed through the full page colour illustrations, as is the joy and pleasure of swimming. Baths have always been places of meeting for conversation and relaxation. Accompa-nying essays comment not only on the architecture but the social and cultural significance of public baths. Amongst the many baths featured are the Art Nouveau Karl- Müller-Volksbad (Public Baths) in Munich, the public baths 'Am Plarrer' in Nuremberg, the indoor baths Elisabethstrasse in Aachen and the Vierodtbad in Karlsruhe.

Hardback 1 85490 387 X
£32.00, DM78.00, $45.00
120 pages, 80 illustrations, 60 colour
September 1994.

First published in 1982, the second edition of this dynamic and thought provoking book has been a standard for many architectural students and profes-sionals. Displayed here are fascinating frame by frame descriptions of an architectural inquest, the 'transcripts'. In addition to a compelling introduction and the fascinating series of drawn architectural thoughts or 'transcripts', the new edition will feature further 'tran-scripts' and text.

The drawings in *Manhattan Transcripts* are neither real projects nor mere fantasies. These drawings propose to transcribe things normally removed from conventional architectural representation, namely the complex relationship between spaces and the set and the script, between 'type' and 'program', between objects and events. Their implicit purpose is significant for the 20th century.

Hardback 1 85490 3810
£18.95, DM 52.00, $35.00
96 pages, extensively illustrated
April 1994.

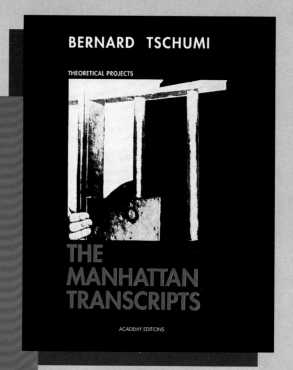

S tarting with his first commissions in the early seventies, the artistic output of Brian Clarke has been extraordinary in its creative range, scope of projects and international appeal. His unique and thorough knowledge of drawings, paintings, gilding, mosaic, calligraphy, heraldry, tapestries, and stained glass has propelled him to see various concepts of artistic mediums as essential and integrated parts of a unified architectural structure. Applying his many talents to a number of architectural challenges, including set designs for the ballet and concerts, his designs can be seen throughout the world.

His design projects, frequently in stained glass, include the new Synagogue in Darmstadt, Germany; Lake Sagami Country Club in Yamanashi, Japan; assorted shopping centres, corporations, and restaurants; Stansted Airport in England; stage sets for Paul McCartney's World Tour and for a tribute to Rudolf Nureyev.

When designing, Clarke keeps the function and theme of a project very much in mind; synthesising them by combining information about light, space and function.

Paperback 1 85490 343 8
£19.95, DM57.00, $35.00
128 pages, over 100 colour illustrations
September 1994

W hile the final product of an architect's efforts typically receives the majority of media attention, the process by which it is achieved is rarely revealed. *Architecture in Process* presents the fascinating sketches, drawings and models produced by the offices of Eric Owen Moss, Morphosis, Steven Holl, Itsuko Hasegawa and Will Alsop who all place considerable emphasis on the evolution of a design idea and the careful documentation of its incremental growth. Each of these talented architects approaches the task differently, providing an intriguing and informative study of the variety of methods now being used to achieve architecture of the highest standard throughout the world. The techniques presented range from the extremely unstructured and informal to the rigorous and definitive, but in each case provide an invaluable insight into the elusive and hitherto intangible process by which architects transform concepts into form.

Paperback 1 85490 306 3
£17.95, DM49.00, $30.00
144 pages, over 200 illustrations,
mainly in colour
May 1994

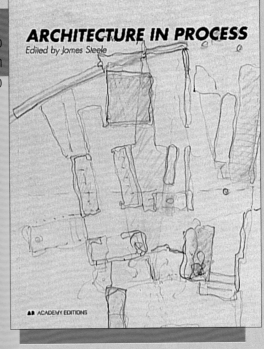

Further information can be obtained from Academy Group Ltd. Tel: 071 402 2141 Fax: 071 723 9540

JAMES GOWAN
by Fred Scott

This exhibition occurs in the season of the London architectural schools' shows, and contrasts with most of the content and preoccupations of the student work in these shows. For many years now, the work from the schools has tended to be fragmentary, complex, episodic and embroiled in process. In contrast James Gowan's drawings appear singular, complete and autonomous.

The contents of the exhibition are arranged chronologically clockwise from the entrance in the three wall cabinets, but beginning in the middle of the room with a drawing displayed flat from his final year at Kingston. This is of an interior perspective of a house for a sculptor: Isokon chair in the foreground beyond this a screen of columns and a transparent sliding wall into a court enclosed by what might be a random terrazzo wall, a picture very much of its time. The beginning of the mannered Modernist investigations among a generation of British architects which lead to Brutalism and to the Leicester engineering building of which he is co-author. One might expect, with the chronological organisation the contents of the exhibition to record or at least form a commentary on the architectural history of the last four decades or so, but this is not the case. After Leicester, and even in some cases, before it, the work becomes less related to its times or to any other time, and more interested in the opposite of fashion and things temporal. This interest is pursued with persistence rather than obsession, by re-drawing projects and buildings, employing a generally interrogative mode. The pictures, for they tend to be this rather than drawings, have an hermetic air – private productions from deepest Bayswater, 'chamber works' so to speak. The projects tend to be explored out of context usually by employing axonometric projection to objectify and isolate the building. The use of this projection from above presents the roof as the primary face, with two facades hanging down and away from it. The roof of course is usually unseen in the everyday, but, on the other hand usually is the clearest

manifestation of the plan. Consequently this choice of projection is particularly congenial to an enquiry between the abstract and the actual.

The detachment from context of the drawing is not merely spatial, but sometimes also cultural and temporal. The Creek Road housing in Greenwich is shown transported to a desert setting; not to the familiar air-conditioned Airstream America Deserta, but to the stereotyped strangeness of a desert from National Geographic complete with camels and wrapped Bedouins. In a more recent picture, the hospital at Rozzano is cut out and collaged as if it were a great country house in what looks like a Repton picturesque landscape. One may discern from this the architects own selection of drawings, an interest in qualities which are immune from compromise and changing fashion, detached even from typology. Seeing Creek Road as it is today, who can blame him for that?

Is context a distraction to true architectural principles? Is its importance over rated? Certainly, with few exceptions, buildings remain where they are put, unless and until they are demolished. The pictures in this exhibition would seem to claim a certain totality and autonomy for the building, a quality associated more readily with product design and works of art. Perhaps the more proper questions are does a work of art require autonomy? Does context always imply incompleteness?

There are many notable drawings, among them, the Churchill College competition entry from the Stirling and Gowan days, which is in the time and again tradition of British competitions of placing the best as runner-up. The Hanningfield section shows components, done in response to a comment about modernity and about which the architect said, 'The house is always the same, it is just that in different ages, different parts are offered up to it.'

The sectioned perspective of the Hackney warehouse demonstrates his desire to impart through proportion and a directness of detailing, a sense of grace to ordinary things. If one looks closely at this apparently precisely drawn perspective the hand drawn quality of the line suddenly reveals itself, and the drawing takes on a different sense, evocative of those early hand-made Modernist objects which were meant to simulate machine production, but constructed with a devotion and cargo cult intensity which the machine was never able to equal.

The one brush with temporality is equally interesting. The Trafalgar Road scheme of 1968 is imagined at some time in the future, under tenant control as I remember the architect once explaining, having been gratified by the tenants adhering strictly to the regulating lines of the facade.

The exhibition is accompanied by a publication of writings and drawings which despite a certain clumsiness or haste in its production, serves to remind one of James Gowan's rare skills as a writer. In particular the book includes the transcript of his 'Details' lecture given at Art Net in 1976, and the review of Colin Rowe's Mathemat-

ics of the Ideal Villa which matches the brilliance of the original. Rowe's essay transcends the dilemma (or dialectic, as some would have it) of whether architectural purpose is to replace or recapture the past. This was a lesson not lost on the reviewer. The Palladian villa drawing with the strange pipework Vitruvian figure in the foreground is included, but apart from this, there is some evidence of a slight self censoring of the quirkier drawings; the Millbank dog for instance, is not in the exhibition, although it appears briefly as an end piece in the catalogue. This section tends to add to an air of renunciation, and to obscure the waywardness of thought which regularly enlivens his unique intelligence.

These pictures, drawings and sketches need to be considered with the architect's built work and his writings in order to clearly understand the particular niche he alone occupies in architectural culture. These sometime seeming straightforward drawings are arrived at by complex means.

STYLE AND CONFIGURATION
JAMES GOWAN

AD ACADEMY EDITIONS · **ES** ERNST & SOHN

ARCHITECTURE & FILM

DANIEL LIBESKIND, NÜRNBERG OPERA SET DESIGN

Architectural Design

ARCHITECTURE & FILM

PETER GREENAWAY, *THE BELLY OF AN ARCHITECT*; *OPPOSITE*: FRITZ LANG, *METROPOLIS*

ACADEMY EDITIONS · LONDON

Acknowledgements

All material is courtesy of the authors and architects unless otherwise stated.
We should like to thank all contributors to this issue, especially Michael Dear and the members of ADOBE LA (Ulises Diaz, Ignacio Fernandez, Gustavo Leclerc, Alessandro Moctezuma and Elpido Rocha). Current pojects include La Posado (a homeless shelter) and Cultural Explainers (three portable public art monuments on community memory); work on p10 was executed using Apple Macintosh and RasterOps imaging technologies; original footage was assembled using a SONY Hi8 video camera); The British Film Institute for its research and reprinting of filmic material, and granting copyright for *Metropolis*; Nadine Covert, Director and Editor of *Architecture on Screen* compiled by the Program for Art on Film in association with The Metropolitan Museum of Art and the J Paul Getty trust, for her interest and assistance; Dennis Davidson Associates for its help in viewing and obtaining slides from *The Hudsucker Proxy* and Polygram Film International for stills (© 1994 Warner Bros; p6); Jennifer Sebree at Universal City Plaza for her interest and assistance with regard to *Jungle Fever*; Spike Lee and 40 Acres for the use of a still from *Jungle Fever* (p7); Peter Greenaway's office for the use of stills from *The Belly of an Architect* (p3); Ziva Freiman from *Progressive Architecture* for her research; Kathy Lendech at Turner Entertainment for granting copyright to *The Fountainhead* and *Mr Blandings Builds His Dream House* (© 1948 RKO Pictures, Inc. All rights reserved; p7); and Vivian Constantinopoulos for her work on Nikos Georgiadis' text. We should also like to thank the following for supplying filmic material, although not all used: United International Pictures for stills from *Intersection* (© 1994 Paramount; p7); Artificial Eye Film Company Ltd for a still from *The Draughtsman's Contract* and *Close My Eyes*; Warner Bros for stills from *Fearless*; Columbia Tristar Home Video for stills from *Sleepless in Seattle*

Front Cover: Coop Himmelb(l)au, detail from the UFA Cinema Centre, Dresden; *Inside Covers*: Westfourth Architecture PC, computer image from the International Centre for Film and Television, Bucharest

Photographic Credits
Front cover and pp48-55 Tom Bonner; p8 Daly, Genik Architects; p10 Robert Flick/Krull Gallery; p11 Figures 4 & 5 Julie Easton (artist: Wiro); p12 Figure 6 Gustavo Leclerc (artist: Wiro); Figure 7 artist: Manuel Cruz; Figure 8 Ruben Oritz-Torres; p13 Figure 9 Ulises Diaz (artist: Peter Padilla) Inner City Murals Project; Figure 10 Ulises Diaz; p14 Figure 11 Julie Easton; p15 Figure 12 Wolch/Dear; Figure 13 M Dear; pp, 7, 16, 18, 19 © 1949 Turner Entertainment Co. All rights reserved; pp1, 20, 21, 37 © British Film Institute; p56 Andrew Bush (view of centre conference room); pp84-85 Carlos Dominguez; pp88-89 © Walt Disney Company; p92 Tom Bonner

EDITOR: Maggie Toy
EDITORIAL TEAM: Iona Spens, Katherine MacInnes, Mark Lane
ART EDITOR: Andrea Bettella CHIEF DESIGNER: Mario Bettella DESIGNER: Laurence Scelles

CONSULTANTS: Catherine Cooke, Terry Farrell, Kenneth Frampton, Charles Jencks
Heinrich Klotz, Leon Krier, Robert Maxwell, Demetri Porphyrios, Kenneth Powell, Colin Rowe, Derek Walker

.First published in Great Britain in 1994 by *Architectural Design* an imprint of
ACADEMY GROUP LTD, 42 LEINSTER GARDENS, LONDON W2 3AN
Member of the VCH Publishing Group
ISBN: 1-85490-246-6 (UK)

Architectural Design Profile 112 is published as part of *Architectural Design* Vol 64 11-12/1994
Architectural Design Magazine is published six times a year and is available by subscription

Distributed to the trade in the United States of America by
ST MARTIN'S PRESS, 175 FIFTH AVENUE, NEW YORK, NY 10010

Printed and bound in Italy

Contents

NIKOS GEORGIADIS, OPEN AIR CINEMA PROJECT

ARCHITECTURAL DESIGN PROFILE No 112

ARCHITECTURE & FILM

MAGGIE TOY
EDITORIAL

Whether real or imaginary there is an inextricable link between the creation of films and the development of our built environment, at least in the exploration of volumetric space in time. Although we are experiencing a time when architects like many others are casting about for new theoretical compasses, architecture is perceived as fragmented, mediated space and thus the assessment is not a new one although it has found new impetus. The connection is explored within this issue with a correspondence between architecture and film. The actual experience of architectural space by an observer within that space has many similarities to the viewer's perception of a chosen sequence within a film. Although the observer may take any chosen direction and appreciate the gratification of other senses, the viewer follows a predetermined route but can see the same as the observer and can gain from the experience. In both cases, a reality is proposed and the imagination is left to fill in the gaps, the key difference is the element of control. Filmmakers have the ability to encourage you to appreciate a building in a different way.

Filmmaker/scriptwriter turned architect/master planner Rem Koolhaas has considered that he is – in a way – still a scriptwriter: 'there is surprisingly little difference between one activity and the other . . . I think the art of the scriptwriter is to conceive sequences of episodes which build suspense and a chain of events . . . the largest part of my work is montage . . . spatial montage'. And this is precisely the beauty of many films which feature the built environment, they have the power to influence viewers' perception and perhaps even to invoke a desire for an improved architectural environment. However we must also appreciate and observe the distinctions between architecture and film and thus avoid the dangers of dwelling on their similarities. The marked differences are continually obvious in the creation of sets without the limitation of reality to contend with and where imagination can be dramatically implemented.

Through a discussion of a world described by the constant exchange between architecture and film via the increased use of perfecting technology, Hani Rashid and Lise Anne Couture isolate familiar situations and encourage the appreciation of the bizarre which already exists

– the exchange between film and technology which is in our everyday lives. The interplay between reality and imagination is explored in *Blade Runner* by Andrew Benjamin to demonstrate the exchange and confusion between representation and reality. The resulting, frightening assessment is brought to a head with the attempted retiring of the humanoids. Architecture and the urban environment have an extremely powerful role in the depiction of a mood and position of the film. *Blade Runner* succeeds in setting a particular scene. Another recent example is *The Hudsucker Proxy* where much of the imagery is centred around the consciousness of space and its relation in time, the power of the architectural spatial tool is maximised. The film's mood is set by the set designer and the urban environment that is created.

The process of viewing architecture is keenly documented by photographers who manipulate and create sometimes misleading single images. With moving film, the stills run at 24 frames/second thus capturing the building being viewed in a closer to 'real' manner. Arguing from the premise that architecture is, at best, a celebration of space, Murray Grigor chronicles the representation of architecture on film, both from the factual documentation point of view and the representation of great masters in the classic *The Fountainhead*. For many years the character of Howard Roark in *The Fountainhead* set an ideal prototype for the architect's role and character. It seems the basic has changed little. Architect equals cult figure of the 90s; when filmmakers want their characters to demonstrate a sense of determination, drive, direction, passion, self-motivation and perhaps a certain sense of arrogance, the suitable profession is that of an architect. Perhaps in the near future a female will fill these shoes. Unfortunately, the use of a female architect has only been taken up by the slightly meeker, secondary roles. We can read a lot about our society when, through its cultural representation on screen, there are few women being portrayed in this positive manner.

Unlike architects, filmmakers can test the popularity of their work by how many people attend a viewing. Architecture is often forced on its users. Perhaps Virtual Reality can offer a choice in the ultimate correspondence between architecture and film.

OPPOSITE: The Hudsucker Proxy, *1994; FROM ABOVE:* Mr Blandings Builds His Dream House, *1948,* The Fountainhead, *1949,* Jungle Fever, *1991,* Intersection, *1994*

8

MICHAEL DEAR
BETWEEN ARCHITECTURE AND FILM[1]

Space, one might say, is nature's way of preventing everything from happening in the same place. In this essay, I shall consider the relationship between geography (the 'science' of space) and the two 'spatial arts' – architecture and film. According to Vidler, the 'complex question of film's architectural role is once again on the agenda'.[2] In truth, it has never been off, but instead simply submerged under a periodic welter of competing ideas. One thinks, for instance, of the cyclical rediscovery of Eisenstein's film theory, or of how film decor was a regular topic in the 1920s/30s' architectural mainstream.[3] Vidler goes on to assert that of all the arts, 'it is architecture that has had the most privileged and difficult relationship to film'.[4] While this may be true, there seems to me to be an unmistakable asymmetry in the ways the two disciplines approach each other; specifically, although architects frequently appeal to the filmic in their theory and practice, the converse is not always true of filmmakers and critics. I explore this asymmetry in more detail in what follows, considering the role of architecture in film and films in architecture. But I shall focus most attention on the possibilities of bridging the two spatial arts via concepts of time and space and the discipline of geography.

> All architecture . . . configures form and material in spatial constructs with ideological force. All architecture . . . politicizes space.
> *Andrea Kahn*[5]

In architectural theory, practice and criticism, there is a long pedigree of reference to film. For example, Ingersoll claims that 'Architecture is the latent subject of almost every movie';[6] and Ramirez leaves no doubt that the architecture of film is 'absolutely central to an understanding of what . . . is happening in contemporary design'.[7] Analogous enthusiasms are to be found in critical studies; for instance, Fischer places architects on a par with directors and actors in German Expressionist movies.[8] And many practising architects have sought to work in both mediums. Perhaps, unsurprisingly, such interaction is especially prominent in the work of contemporary architects in Los Angeles, including *inter alia* Craig Hodgetts and Hsin-Ming Fung, Anton Furst and Frank Israel.

In a concise historical overview, Vidler reveals the parallel evolution of modernism in architec-

ture and film. A distinct theoretical apparatus that emerged at the beginning of the twentieth century posited architecture as the 'fundamental site of film practice ... and, at the same time, posited film as the modernist art *par excellence* – a vision of the fusion of space and time.'[9] Abel Gance, writing in 1912, anticipated a new synthesis of the movement of space and time, but it was Elie Faure who first coined the term 'cineplastics', to bring together the two aesthetics. Ultimately, this would give rise to the totalising plasticity of German Expressionism, most notably in Robert Weine's *Das Kabinett des Dr Caligari* (1919). From the mid-1920s, the more purely decorative and staged characteristics of Expressionist film were denounced, and a trend toward greater realism evolved. The subsequent emphasis on physical reality led Erwin Panofsky to announce the unique possibilities of film, 'defined as *dynamization of space* and accordingly, *spatialization of time*.'[10]

At present, architects (like many others) are casting about for new theoretical compasses, in what is likely to be an extended period of post-Enlightenment uncertainty. Though the genealogy of this rebirth is somewhat obscure, already slivers of a new synthesis are emerging, crystal-like, from the proliferation of critical studies. The thrust of this synthesis is, I believe, toward a more 'grounded' theory and practice of architecture. As critics begin to pore over the piles of conceptual corpses, hostilities and putative hegemonies become more overt.

The contemporary era has, for instance, witnessed an efflorescence of interest in the relationship between architecture and film, undoubtedly tied to the emergence of revitalised cultural studies and the rise of a video culture. There also seems to be much consensus that Post-Modernism's demise was heralded with an almost indecent haste, and deconstructivism (that ill-fated hybrid) never caught on. Jim Collins rues the disintegration of the Post-Modern project, which has been reduced to 'designer tea kettles or flattened into coffee table books of simulated theory about America.'[11] In the meantime, others reach back to earlier verities for inspiration. The 'new urbanism' – described by one of its advocates as 'focused to the point of evangelism'[12] – seeks to re-install garden-city principles to the design of suburbs.

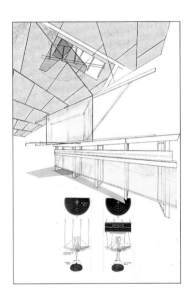

OPPOSITE AND ABOVE: Figures 1 & 2, Conversion to Projection Facility, University of Southern California, Los Angeles, Architects: Daly, Genik, Completion August 1994.
The conversion involves the creation of space that is simultaneously more generic and more singular than the existing condition. The project seeks to explore the inverse and complementary relationship between architectural space and film space. The project addresses the architectural qualities of optical phenomena, as they are made evident by the process of projection and subsequent reflection. The room, with a reflective ceiling, is developed as a spectral envelope that behaves as a three-dimensional screen. It is constantly modified by the circumstances of projection and adjusted by the material conditions of the room

The lugubrious cries of these (Ebenezer) Howardists have been offset by those who seek a greater emphasis on context in architectural thinking. For instance, in his preface to an important collection of architectural texts, Bernard Tschumi makes clear that: 'The history of architecture is as much in the history of its writings as its buildings.'[13] Critic Herbert Muschamp has consistently argued that social and spatial forms are more intimately linked than architects usually acknowledge (through what geographers term the 'sociospatial dialectic'). In his analysis of Queer Space, Muschamp highlights the transgressive nature of gay communities, warning that norms simultaneously define 'abnorms'. He excoriates architects for spending too much time on symbolic forms at the expense of grappling with political and economic realities.[14] A poignant echo for a grounded theory is offered in Charles Jencks' post-riot meditation on Los Angeles. Urging us to promote (not simply accommodate) the emerging diversity of cities, Jencks points to the futility of asking art or architecture to compensate for political, economic or social inequity.[15] Andrea Kahn is equally blunt: 'to attend to the work of architecture we must first seek out what we do not see – that the art of construction goes beyond appearances . . . our work is not simply a matter of drawing and following the line.'[16]

> The power of the film image to (mis)represent the material and social world lies . . . in its ability to blur the boundaries of space and time, reproduction and simulation, reality and fantasy, and to obscure the traces of its own ideologically based production.
> *Jeff Hopkins*[17]

The history of film, in its turn, is replete with references to architecture. Eisenstein's classic work identified two paths of the 'spatial eye':

> the cinematic, where a spectator follows an imaginary line among a series of objects . . . 'diverse impressions passing in front of an immobile spectator' – and the architectural, where 'the spectator moved through a series of carefully disposed phenomena which he absorbed in order with his visual sense.[18]

Despite this early conflation of the two spatial arts, it is doubtful whether or not a true exchange has occurred between architecture and film.[19]

Take, for instance, Kahn's critique of Tati's *Playtime* (1965). In this film, she claims, architecture has a starring role. Yet she is clear how Tati constructed his cinematic Paris:

> Tati builds his city, unmistakably the city of Paris, not through recognizable monuments but through unmistakable movements . . . The set (buildings) is without character, but the space of action is teeming with site specificity. Architecture, we learn, supports but cannot purport place.[20]

Ingersoll adds to my burgeoning sense of the alienation between film and architecture: 'Film demands that architecture only serve the plot, and *thus there are no constraints on structure or space.*'[21] It would be hard to imagine a more surgical separation between architecture and film – all except the most abstract of architectures is inevitably place-bound; but cinematic conventions are aggressively committed to the compression, expansion and even reversal of time-space contexts.

Contemporary film studies have gone far beyond architecture for their referents, drawing from structuralism, semiotics, psychoanalysis, post-modernism and deconstruction, as well as from popular culture (especially video and rap music). Yet, as in architecture, we encounter in film an analogous uncertainty, a loss of theoretical moorings. Denzin claims Post-Modernism as a 'cinematic age', but is critical of cinematic representations of Post-Modernism, which fail to offer 'anything more than superficial solutions to the present conditions'.[22] (Think, for instance, of the 'happy endings' in Ridley Scott's original *Blade Runner*, 1982, and his *Thelma and Louise*, 1991). At the core of this discontent is the issue of representation.

Nothing in the world is fixed or immutable. The space of the film is, at the limit, the frame that passes the eye 24 times every second. The composition and content of each frame are nonrandom decisions, but (as with any text) the artist cannot control the effects that each framing produces. Thus, the quality of authenticity in representation is inherently unstable – which is, of course, precisely the characteristic that most filmmakers deliberately seek to exploit; and, by extension, of central significance is the power of the spectator to experience a film *critically*, to engage in what Derrida described as an 'incessant movement of recontextualization'.[23]

The most sustained effort to connect film (and architecture) with the ambiguities of Post-Modern culture has been made by Fredric Jameson. Three concepts are central in his project:[24] the *political unconscious* which identifies the often opaque articulation between the economic base and cultural forms; *Post-Modernism* being the cultural dominant of the current phase of late capitalism; and *cognitive mapping* the intersection between the social and the political explaining how individuals learn about, and function in, social space. Jameson focuses on the intrinsic spatiality of filmic representation and the hegemony of cinematic images in our political unconscious. He stresses, along with Michel Foucault and others, how we have moved from a Modernist obsession with time/history to a Post-Modern epoch of space/geography.

OPPOSITE: Figure 3, Segment of 'Parade Route', Pasadena, May 8-9, 1993.
Parade Route visually traces the itinerary of the annual Tournament of the Roses Parade in Pasadena, California. The route bisects a broad range of cultural, socioeconomic and ecological phenomena, providing a visual inventory . . . I do not see in isolated, distinctly framed moments; rather, I see in connected, layered occurrences in time. I see many things collectively creating a sense of place. I use the systematic display and logic of the camera to render what is out there. The camera and lens frame only a segment of the continuity that is before it. If I move only a little before I make the next exposure, part of the previous image and part of what is next to it will coexist. The connection between the parts of the two frames will suggest continuity and movement. But at the same time, because of the repetition, something new is created. A thing that only occurred once now occurs twice and the possibility for the manipulation of perception and the creation of a fiction has begun (Robert Flick); FROM ABOVE: Figures 4 & 5, ADOBE LA (see caption on p13)

11

Space is never empty; it always embodies a meaning.
Henri Lefebvre[25]

Contemporary human geography is that part of social theory which focuses on the spatial patterns and processes that underlie the structures and appearances of everyday life. Human behaviour is both enabled and constrained by a complex set of sociocultural, political and economic processes acting across time and space; at issue is how we explain the variety of the resultant time-space 'fabric'. Social process operates at different scales (from global to local), and is mediated through the interactions of deep-seated structures, their institutional forms and the actions of individual human agents. There is also a time dimension, since 'place' is a complex amalgam of past, present and emergent forms coexisting simultaneously in a single landscape. In a most fundamental sense, therefore, the central task of what I term the 'geographical puzzle' is to *understand the simultaneity of time and space* in structuring social process; human geography is the study of contemporaneity of social processes through time and space. By extension, one purpose of architecture (plus urban planning) and film-making is to *forge new time-space relationships*.

The time-space articulations proposed in geography may be useful in reconnecting architecture and film studies. I want to sketch the beginnings of such a connection in the remainder of this essay, starting with the characterisation of the Derridean perspective:

Once spacing is introduced, as a sine qua non of linguistic expression and of sense-making processes in general, then the philosopher of language necessarily becomes a philosopher of spatial articulation(s). The task becomes, in effect, an architectural one, mapping out the limits and testing the boundaries of communicational space, or that of a plastic artist, exploring the relations among line, form, and shades of meaning.[26]

Derrida shows how language, in its material form of writing (and drawing), always entails a spacing (*espacement*) that works at one remove from its author. I believe that this spacing, or 'distancing' dynamic is a key to articulating the related spatialisations in architecture and film [Figs 1 and 2]. I can show this in a preliminary way through a series of examples. Rather than expressing an entire problematic, these examples suggest how the spaces between architecture and film can be profitably articulated through the middle ground of geography.

In film, the distance between observer and observed is primarily created by the camera. Kracauer suggested that 'distance is necessary to lessen the shock that would result from the spectator's direct confrontation with certain

phenomena'.[27] The case of pornography is illustrative of a broader paradox, however. Here, the camera:

plays off a certain fear of crudity, coarseness, and undisguised, unsublimated sexuality. Only through the image can the observer confront that which would otherwise frighten . . . In the case of pornographic cinema, the camera becomes a device for creating distance and the medium of a harmless voyeurism.[78]

The paradoxical power of the filmic dialectic is clear: on one hand, the camera distances; on the other, it invites the observer in. In the anti-pornography documentary *Not a Love Story* (Bonnie Sherr Klein, 1981), the camera self-consciously, simultaneously seduces and repels the viewer as it confronts the nature of pornographic representation. It is easy to appreciate the potential of the video revolution which has made observers out of those who were previously observed, and thus dramatically altered the power of prior distancing dynamics.

The inherent spatiality of the voyeuristic camera is evident in Natter's discussion of Walter Ruttman's *Berlin, Symphony of a Great City* (1927). As well as in the framing of a scene, he argues that the difference between a shot (an uninterrupted sequence of film time) and a cut (an instantaneous change from one shot to another) thoroughly defines film as spatial. The importance of scale as an element of filmic spatiality is also revealed in the connection between close-up and medium- and long-shots. The essential translation from real-world place to cinematic space is, according to Natter, 'marked not by repetition, but by alterity, whose visual element is the fragment'.[29]

Architecture is also experienced as a fragmentary, mediated space. In our transportation-oriented culture, one important distance-related variable is speed. Los Angeles, the archetypal autopia, is a 'punctual rather than linear urbanism', meant to be read from a passing car [Fig 3].[30] At its extreme, however, speed has been fetishised into a kind of perceptual dominant, as in Boyer: 'It is speed that has erased the fragmentation and hierarchies of space and time, homogenized everything to an absolute present.'[31] But the absence of speed is also an element of place-making. Michel de Certeau has drawn attention to the importance of walking as a spatial practice, constitutive of people's life paths. And in Latino cultures, low-riders (carefully decorated cars) drive slowly through neighbourhoods so that they and their occupants may be seen. In shopping malls, too, people are constitutive of the scene. In Agrest's terms: 'Fashion transforms people into objects, linking street and theater through one aspect of their common ritual nature.'[32] In other words,

OPPOSITE: Figures 6, 7 & 8, ADOBE LA; FROM ABOVE: Figures 9 & 10. Latino Public Art, Los Angeles (ADOBE LA – Architects and Designers Opening the Border Edge of Los Angeles).
A collaborative Latino group dedicated to visual documentation of the Latino presence in LA, and to creating work and resources in collaboration with the community.
The four initial manifestations of Latino cultural landscapes are: Spirituality in the Landscape – religious expressions in the form of altars in homes, garden shrines and images on walls (ie the Virgen de Guadalupe). These markers of history and culture are brought by immigrants and express identity in the new homeland. Barrio Art – outward expressions, including murals, decorations on cars and tattoos, which become fixed or mobile elements of the landscape, communicating visually with an entire neighbourhood. Coded Messages: Graffiti and Tagging – often controversial as they are viewed as vandalism; yet they reflect the social conditions and aspirations of Latino youth. Art of Survival: Street Vendors and Taco Trocas – street vendors ranging from solitary fruit-sellers on freeway off-ramps to decorated trucks, on which images often represent churches or villages in Mexico or mythical characters from popular songs

everyone and everything becomes part of the aesthetics of the commodity system.

The theoretical linkage between film and architectural space is captured in Maureen Turim's 'displacement' process: 'Not just abstractionism, but an act of visual de-centering and symbolic displacement; it is in these terms that we can describe the interaction between architecture and the cinematic apparatus in avant-garde films.'[33] The displacement/distancing principle is part of a wider epistemological puzzle. Iain Chambers, discussing the possibilities of criticising the present, argued for immersing oneself in the local at the same time as observing from a distance. In his case, distance is provided through the lens of theory. Both local immersion and a more distant theoretical stance are needed for understanding. This explains why, in a polyvocal discourse, many avowed Post-Modernists have embraced the challenge of

standpoint theories (most notably feminism) as a way of achieving distance.

In political terms, distance means difference. Los Angeles, where Jencks claims to have observed 'more sheer difference' than any other city he knows, is a city in crisis.[34] To save our future, he turns to Charles Taylor, who modified the potentially divisive 'politics of difference' to a more positive 'politics of recognition'. Such a strategy, Jencks believes, will encourage the development of separate identities, and place-making based on diversity – something already manifest in Los Angeles' heteropolis [Figs 4-11].[35] A new language of difference would also be needed, allowing for a discursive heterogeneity in political, professional and intellectual life. The tasks of unpacking and reforming these complicated archaeologies of place take on a new urgency in an era of increasing socioeconomic inequality and political unrest [Figs 12 and 13].

Notes

1 I am grateful to the artists and architects who helped me in the preparation of this essay, especially those who provided examples of their work to illustrate my argument. Rob Wilton provided valuable research assistance. Thanks also to Dana Cuff, Kevin Daly, Ulises Diaz, Robbert Flick, Chris Genik, Ignacio Hernandez, Gustavo Leclerc, and Jennifer Wolch for good advice.

2 Anthony Vidler, 'The Explosion of Space: Architecture and the Filmic Imaginary', *Assemblage*, 21, 1993, p 45.

3 Richard Ingersoll, 'Cinemarchitecture' *Design Book Review*, Spring 1992, p 7.

4 Vidler, *op cit*, note 2, p 45.

5 Andrea Kahn, 'The Invisible Mask', *Drawing/Building/Text: Essays in Architectural Theory*, edited by Andrea Kahn, Princeton Architectural Press, New York, 1991, p 104.

6 Ingersoll, *op cit*, note 3, p 5.

7 Juan Antonio Ramírez, 'Ten Lessons (or Commandments) about Architecture and the Cinema', *Design Book Review*, Spring 1992, p 9.

8 Volker Fischer, 'Le Decor, Element de Psychogramme sur l'Architecture dans le Film Expressioniste', *Images et Imaginaires d'Architecture*, Centre National d'Art et de Culture George Pompidou, Paris, 1984, p 110.

9 Vidler, *op cit*, note 2, p 46.

10 *ibid*, p 50; emphases in original.

11 Jim Collins, 'A Clear Vista of the Edge of Civilization: Urbanism, Mass Culture and True Stones', *Cinema and Architecture*, Iris, Paris, 1991, p 127.

12 Daniel Solomon, 'Rallying around the New Urbanism', *Places*, 9(1), 1994, p 74. An overview of the new urbanism is to be found in Peter Katz, *The New Urbanism: Toward an Architecture of Community*, McGraw Hill, New York, 1994.

13 Bernard Tschumi, 'Foreword', *Architecture Culture 1943-1968*, edited by Joan Ockman, Columbia/Rizzoli, New York, 1993, p 11.

14 Herbert Muschamp, 'Designing a Framework for Diversity', *New York Times*, June 19, 1994, p 34.

15 Charles Jencks, Heteropolis: *Los Angeles, the Riots, and the Strange Beauty of Hetero-Architecture*, Academy Editions, London, 1993, p 103.

16 Andrea Kahn, 'Playtime with Architects', *Design Book Review*, Spring 1992, p 29.

17 Jeff Hopkins, 'A Mapping of Cinematic Places', *Place, Power, Situation and Spectacle: A Geography of Film*, edited by Stuart Aitken and Leo Zonn, Rowman and Littlefield, Lanham, Maryland, 1994, p48.

18 Quoted in Vidler, *op cit*, note 2, p 56.

19 Ben Gibson, 'Architecture et Cinema', *Images et Imaginaires d'Architecture, op cit*, note 8, p 113. But see also Donald Albrecht, *Designing Dreams: Modern Architecture in the Movies*, Harper and Row, New York, 1986.

20 Andrea Kahn, *op cit*, note 16, p 27, emphasis added.

21 Ingersoll, *op cit*, note 3, p 5, emphasis added.

22 Norman Denzin, *Images of Postmodern Society: Social Theory and Contemporary Cinema* Sage, Publications, Newbury Park, 1991, pp 150, 155.

23 Wolfgang Natter, 'The City as Cinematic Space: Modernism and Place in *Berlin, Symphony of a Great City*', in Aitken and Zonn, *op cit*, note 19, p 205.

24 Fredric Jameson, *The Geopolitical Aesthetic: Cinema and Space in the World System*, Indiana University Press, Bloomington, 1992, pp x-xv.

25 Henri Lefebvre, *The Production of Space*, Blackwell, Oxford, 1991, p 154.

26 This discussion of the work of Derrida appears in Peter Brunette and David Wills (eds), *Deconstruction and the Visual Arts: Art, Media, Architecture*, Cambridge University Press, Cambridge, 1994, p 3.

27 Quoted in Gertrude Koch, 'The Body's Shadow Realm', *Dirty Looks: Women, Pornography, Power*, edited by

ABOVE: Figure 11, ADOBE LA (see p13); OPPOSITE ABOVE: Figure 12, preliminary sketch: Self-governing Outdoor Living Facility (SOLF) for Homeless People.

Designed as an off-street living space for between 25 and 40 people, the SOLF anticipates relocating an existing street encampment to a secure site with individual shelter/sleeping spaces plus shared bathroom, cooking and storage facilities. Community members would be responsible for their own governance, including resident admissions and terminations, allocation of community maintenance chores and policing of behavioural or substance misuse problems

Pamela Church Gibson and Roma Gibson, BFI Publishing, London, 1993, p 37.

28 *ibid*, p 37.

29 Natter, *op cit,* note 23, p 211.

30 Joseph Giovanni, 'LA Architects: they did it their way', *Los Angeles Times Magazine,* May 15, 1994, p 32.

31 Christine Boyer quoted in Kahn, *op cit,* note 16, p 28.

32 Diana Agrest, *Architecture from Without,* MIT Press, Cambridge, 1991, p 63.

33 Maureen Turim, 'The Displacement of Architecture in Avant-Garde Films', in *Cinema and Architecture, op cit,* note 11, p 25.

34 Jencks, *op cit,* note 15, p 172.

35 *ibid*, pp 10, 75-7, 109, 118-9. See also Museum of Contemporary Art, *Urban Revisions: Current Projects for the Public Realm,* Museum of Contemporary Art and MIT Press, Cambridge, 1994.

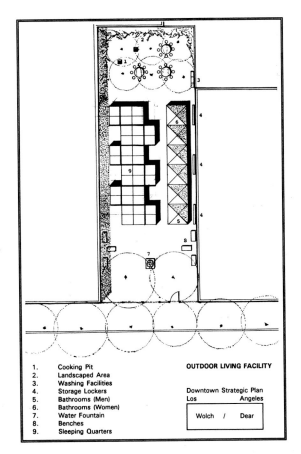

1. Cooking Pit
2. Landscaped Area
3. Washing Facilities
4. Storage Lockers
5. Bathrooms (Men)
6. Bathrooms (Women)
7. Water Fountain
8. Benches
9. Sleeping Quarters

OUTDOOR LIVING FACILITY

Downtown Strategic Plan
Los   Angeles

| Wolch | / | Dear |

Figure 13, Genesis I: village for homeless people, Golden Avenue, Los Angeles, California. Established on the site of a former parking lot near downtown Los Angeles in November 1993, Genesis I is a pilot project initiated by Ted Hayes to assist homeless people to transition out of a street-based existence. Up to 24 people can be housed in the 18 domes, three of which are devoted to communal facilities. The village incorporates many of the SOLF design principles (see ABOVE, Fig 12), including self-governance and a resident core selected from an already-existing street encampment. The novelty of the dome architecture has successfully broken down barriers between homeless and homed

MURRAY GRIGOR
SPACE IN TIME
Filming Architecture

*The depth-plane defies the flat camera-eye.
The essence of organic architecture is space,
space flowing outward, space flowing inward
(not necessarily by the use of the picture-
window).*
Frank Lloyd Wright, A Testament: The
Camera Eye

*The outer edges of the screen are not, as the
technical jargon would seem to imply, the
frame of the film image. They are the edges of
a piece of masking that shows only a portion
of reality. The picture frame polarises space
inwards. On the contrary, what the screen
shows us seems to be part of something
prolonged indefinitely into the universe. A
frame is centripetal, the screen centrifugal.*
André Bazin, What Is Cinema?

At its best, architecture is a celebration
of space. Cinema, on the other hand,
as Jimmy Stewart so well put it, gives
people 'tiny pieces of time'.[1] The idea of filming
architecture seems therefore almost an axiom of
cinema. After all, the marriage began in the
heady days of early Hollywood. The most
memorable movies of the so-called 'silent' era
have such a sense of the built environment that it
would be possible to recreate whole reaches of
early twentieth-century Los Angeles from them.
Should ever one want to wind back the urban
clock to its original state and do a Williamsburg
on the city of the angels, there is all the evidence
needed to replace today's stucco dingbat
junkitecture and reconstruct building after
building along Santa Monica Boulevard. Just
look behind those frenetic Keystone Kops to see
them all recorded in irrefutable context by the
cameras of Mack Sennett.

But what of tomorrow? Are the movies of our
time giving us a similar view into the future?
Does Ridley Scott's *Blade Runner* (1982), with
its bleak vision of a disintegrating Los Angeles,
predict the shape of this great metropolis in the
century to come?

Architecture and Cinema
In the 30s, architecture often 'called the shots' in
movies. The stunning top-of-the-town night-club
set in George Steven's *Swing Time* (1936)
evoked Rockefeller Center's Rainbow Room

which opened in 1934. In *The Fountainhead*
(1949), based on the Ayn Rand novel, the
subject of architecture actually *is* the movie. In
scene after scene, King Vidor hones his architectural filming techniques won from his pioneering days exploring the darker side of
skyscrapers in *The Crowd* (1928). Vidor's
camera sweeps around Edward Carrère's
architectural parodies of Frank Lloyd Wright
buildings, which include an unbelievably
overstretched Falling Water. Invited to create
the buildings and interior spaces, Wright de-
manded a fee of US$250,000, which the studio
declined. However, the master did design a
never-to-be-built home for Ayn Rand to be
called, of course, The Fountainhead. On its
release, the film caused torrents of outrage in
the architectural press, as Donald Albrecht
documents so well in Designing Dreams.[2]

It has always struck me that scholarship
seldom turns its attention to the more immediate
past and nowhere less so than in architecture.
We know far more about the life of the della
Scala family as patrons of the Castelvecchio in
Renaissance Verona than we do about the
shadowy Mr Ennis who gave Wright considerable sums to build his Mayan fortress on a
Hollywood bluff in the 20s.

When researching the skyscraper episode of
'Pride of Place' (the 1985 Mobil/PBS series on
American architecture), we found that it was the
building that influenced the style of the Chrysler
automobile, not the other way round. We heard
that those great stylised Art Deco preying eagle
gargoyles, destined to be Chrysler hood orna-
ments, were the work of a Hollywood set designer. Soon we were talking to the spry designer Cheseley Bonestell, then well into his
nineties, who remembered developing the ideas
of the architect William van Alen. Bonestell also
helped to shape the sky-scraping details of *The
Fountainhead*'s mythical Wynand Building. Why,
one wonders, did the film cause so much fury?

At their most basic level, architecture and
cinema have natural inbuilt affinities. Plan,
construction; script, production – architects and
film directors proceed down parallel routes to
create their works. In the end, is it not with their
sense of architectural space and place that
many of our favourite movies haunt us? After all,
Citizen Kane (1941), most people's all-time

17

favourite movie, devours architecture on a Piranesian scale. The megalomaniac shapes and spaces delivered by Gregg Toland's photography linger in the mind's eye long after Welles' breathless narrative has evaporated in our memory. The same director even saw the spatial possibilities of the Gare d'Orsay for Kafka's *The Trial* (1963), long before this abandoned Paris railroad station turned itself into a museum of nineteenth-century art.

Many film directors, such as Fritz Lang, actually began their careers training as architects. Raymond Durgnat points out that the exuberance of Viennese Baroque architecture, which Carol Reed allows to dominate the squalid action of intrigue in *The Third Man* (1949), ends in the architectural negative – a sewer.[3] In Italy – that country which all architects dream about – Luchino Visconti and Michelangelo Antonioni brought buildings and cities to the heart of their cinema, a tradition that Bernardo Bertolucci imaginatively continues. In *Metropolis* (1926), Lang's nightmarish vision even reduces his extras to architectural decoration by creating vast geometrical reliefs of trudging people. Carl Dreyer, himself an accomplished architectural filmmaker in documentaries such as *The Danish Village Church (Landsbykirken;* 1941), claimed that architecture was cinema's closest relative. Nicholas Ray always held that his love of CinemaScope was due to a few months spent at Frank Lloyd Wright's horizontal world of Taliesin at Spring Green, Wisconsin.[4] The young Ray might also have had his ambitions in cinema encouraged here, for Wright always had his pick of movies playing in his in-house theatre.

A note was found in Wright's papers after his death saying that if a movie was ever to be made on his life he wanted John Huston to direct it, perhaps because Wright had visited Huston in the home the director had designed for himself. Wright was sufficiently impressed with it, apart from criticising the overgenerous ceiling heights, to exclaim that what the world needed most was more amateur architects.

Wright himself was a keen amateur filmmaker. Ironically, Wright's 16mm footage of the Larkin Building in Buffalo, New York, (whip pans of swirling red bricks from tower to tower) constitutes the only film record of that much-lamented masterpiece. A few of his shots are incorporated into my own film on Wright's architecture. These heroic bursts of red never fail to shock an audience into a sense of tragic loss, especially poignant for those who have previously perceived this great twentieth-century building only as dull grey masses in black-and-white photographs in books.

Television and Architecture

Architecture itself is now back on the public agenda as a popular subject for discussion.

New and old buildings are news again. Apart from Wright's Guggenheim Museum in New York, how many modern buildings over the past 50 years have been immortalised on postcards? But now new buildings challenge the standard tourist icons; postcards of the Louvre's pyramid, the East Building of the National Gallery of Art in Washington DC, the Centre Pompidou in Paris, the Sydney Opera House and scores of new German art galleries fly around the world. Have not modern museums and art galleries become the secular cathedrals and pilgrimage centres of our times? With so much public interest in the built environment, why then are films on architecture and architects such a rarity on television today?

One good reason presents itself immediately. Television executives usually come from a journalistic background and find it hard to contemplate programmes on 'pure' architecture. Some senior decision-makers in the media have actually told me that the very idea of making architectural films is doomed because 'buildings don't move'! Add to this the universal problem of our word-driven culture and reporter-style programming. Television as a visual medium is still transmitted to what its controllers call an 'audience.' It has yet to justify the invention of the more appropriate word 'vidience'. Then there is the fear of contemplative silence on television. Contrast this with your experience of exploring architecture. Most of us attempt to escape the chattering tourist guides by sliding away to experience the spaces and the details of a building, to ponder our private thoughts. Finally, there is the strong chance that the television executive will never have heard of your proposed architect or building.

All these formidable factors are stacked against you before you even begin to think about structuring any cinematic approaches to your chosen subject. It is something of a miracle that any film on architecture ever appears on television. How can a filmmaker reveal the significance of an architect's work in a verbal pitch to a funder or television executive?

Show, Don't Tell

Remember that swinging door in Jacques Tati's *Playtime* (1967)? With every swing the name of a different world city appeared on a poster, each with an identical tower block of stacked wall ovens. How much more effective an indictment on the architectural conformity of the so-called International Style than a thousand words from an authoritative talking head.

In schools, architecture is often communicated through photographs. A hundred years ago, infinite care was taken in photographing architecture, particularly interiors. Rising-front cameras, multiple exposures, large-plate

Still from The Fountainhead, *1949*

negative are all combined with the care and mastery of the photographers to capture an almost psychological feeling of particular interior spaces. No one has captured the mystery of Charles Rennie Mackintosh's Glasgow School of Art so well as Bedford Lemere did in his interior photographs of 1904. Perhaps he had the architect by his side, just as I felt I had when I stooped to get a low angle inside Taliesin and passed the first test of the master (according to his assistants) of photographing rooms at chair height.

Nowadays, architecture is the victim of the bug-eyed lens; endless supplies of 24mm-lens shots constitute what most students grasp of contemporary buildings today. This tendency dominates the few programmes on architecture that reach television, where a clutch of wide-shot cutaways bridges a presenter's take or illustrates an architect's discussion of his work.

A brighter tendency is seen in 'Building Sights', a BBC2 television series conceived by Clare Paterson and carried into its sixth series by Ruth Rosenthal. These ten-minute videos, designed as short programme bridges, reach a refreshingly large audience. Each short features a personality from the world of architecture, the arts or literature who presents a building or structure that intrigues them. As would be expected, the videos are at their best with architectural writers or architects at their helm. Jean Nouvel's Arab Institute in Paris was enthusiastically delivered by writer/critic Janet Abrams. Perhaps the most bizarre 'building' was architect Norman Foster's choice of a 747 jumbo jet. Even at their most fragmentary, like the opera singer Brigitte Fassbaender's butterfly approach to the Hundertwasser Haus in Vienna (music while we cut), this series presents unexpected architectural samplers for future curiosity.

Great architecture usually exceeds the expectations generated by a photograph. Since our knowledge of buildings comes from seeing isolated facades (the building as painting) or forms (the building as sculpture), only filming can deliver the essential spatial dimensions of space and volume. To comprehend architecture, one needs to move through its spaces. After all, this is how we all experience buildings, inside and outside: we walk, we look, we pass through space. Perspectives are revealed. Corners turned. Scale changes. The depth dimension is revealed. Details can be explored. A combination of predetermined camera tracks and pre-arranged lighting plans offers a chance to reveal the unfolding of space and vista and show the movement of light on texture.

An opportunity to explore a building along these lines came my way when Jack Coia, one of Scotland's most notable and charismatic architects, refused to be involved in any hagiographical account of his life in a Scottish Arts Council film to celebrate his Gold Medal award from the Royal Institute of Architects. *Space and Light* (1972) therefore became an exploration of one building, Saint Peter's College, Cardross, on the river Clyde. Wrapped around the handsome Scots baronial home of a Clyde shipping magnate, whose trade with the Orient had inspired him to fill the surrounding gardens with Japanese shrubs and trees, the new seminary became the most significant modernist building in Scotland. It clearly reflected the interest of Coia's partners, Andy MacMillan and Isi Metzstein, in the churches of Le Corbusier.

My aim was to follow the activities of the students through a day, using long exploratory shots. Taking the challenge from Ansel Adams (it's not what you see, it's how you look), I realised that everything depended on the precision of the camera moves. Fortunately, Tony Cridlin, who had just finished operating tracking dollies, cranes and even wheelchairs for Stanley Kubrick on *Clockwork Orange* (1971), brought his skills and experience to our little production. The only commentary in the film's seven sections comes from Frank Spedding's musical palimpsest, where the Gregorian chant of *Veni Creator Spiritus* and a Beethoven piano sonata counterpoint the sacred and the secular aspects of the building. The end result can never be matched, as Cardross is now wrecked, gutted as a ruin, the victim of changed dogma and neglect. The short film has become its requiem.

Special Effects and Feature Film Techniques

Apart from attempting to simulate something of the feeling of experiencing architecture, the recent developments in computer-aided design systems, together with the creative leaps of the imagination in the wake of *Star Wars* (1977), have opened up a whole new area for films on architecture. Through spectacular computer-created special effects, Jacques Barsac allows us to fly around Le Corbusier's ultimate megalopolis in his 1987 centenary series on the architect (*Le Corbusier*). More recently, *Masters of Illusion* (1991), a serious but immensely popular exploration of Renaissance perspective using computer-driven sequences, became the top-selling video in the National Gallery in Washington. This combination of the computer skills of Rick Harper, an exponent of Hollywood special effects, and the scholarship of art historian Martin Kemp ushers in a whole new area of programme-making. How instructive it would be for viewers to experience with this technology the development of Wright's grid plan from the simple Froebel Blocks to the complexities of, say, the Larkin Building.

Architectural filmmaking benefits from techniques normally reserved for feature filmmaking.

Still from The Fountainhead, *1949*

19

My experience is that technicians, who are used to spending time on lighting and laying tracks, double their enthusiasm for creative work when they realise that no actors will arrive to impede their hours of labour.

Shooting Frank Lloyd Wright's Los Angeles houses with great Hollywood technicians raised our expectations to a new level. With tracks laid, a fire ablaze in the great hearth of the Ennis House, we all waited for the miracle of that vast disc of the Pacific sun to drop through the palms and throw its orange light and shadows over Wright's patterned blocks. Our celebrations had a pre-Columbian theme that night.

We filmed Falling Water in the cold of winter, in early spring, and in the fall when leaves swirled downwards from the gold- and red-leafed branches twisting above us, as in a Douglas Sirk melodrama. The great cantilevers of Wright's masterpiece were alive in moving coloured shadows. Air, earth and water; only fire was missing to complete the four elements of the medieval quaternary. But in the final sequence there it is. A flicker of flames dissolves through the white water to the great hearth above, as our camera moves back into Wright's great interior. To get so low, flat on the floor's rock slabs in that great living room, we had devised a special lens mount and prism. In the final fusion, Frank Spedding's music would counterpoint the dissolve.

At the recording session, narrator Anne Baxter (Wright's grand-daughter) asked to change a word in the commentary which Tom Heinz and I had worked and reworked. Now Anne had the poolside rock 'shouldering' up beside the hearth. In the end, the sequence seemed to create itself in vision and sound. The effect of the final result would have been impossible to predict in words so many months before.

The Untapped Potential

> I cannot distinguish between thought and feeling, and I am convinced that a combination of words and music, colour and movement can extend human experience in a way that words alone cannot do. For this reason I believe in television as a medium, and was prepared to give up two years writing to see what could be done with it.
>
> *Kenneth Clark: Foreword to* Civilisation[5]

Michael Gill, who brought *Civilisation* (1969) to the screen, remembers his initial discussion with Kenneth Clark on the practicalities of how the BBC television series would be filmed. Britain's most accomplished public speaker in the arts had assumed that he would talk his lecture through in a studio with the appropriate visual sections projected on a screen as he went along. Nothing had prepared him for the great trudge across Europe that Gill and his team prepared for him and which Clark later referred

to as the happiest two years of his life.

The American architectural historian Vincent Scully could provide a similar focal point for an imaginative series on architecture.[6] His legendary bardic reach, his astonishing ability to leap continents in his references, could make a memorable contribution to the presentation of architecture on screen. His lectures at Yale have inspired generations of students who have since become writers, artists, architects or filmmakers (but presumably not television executives since none have shown interest in such a series).[7]

To combine the effect of light on space and texture through movement, to show buildings within their context was the potential implicit in filming the 'Pride of Place' series on American architecture. Crossing the country with the cameraman Terry Hopkins and a crew of feature-filmmaking technicians, with an Aladdin's cave of equipment, enabled us to show more than tell.

My plan was not to illustrate interviews (wide shots or zooms between the questions) but to attempt to reveal the buildings within their context, to show their interior spaces and details always with a sense of scale. Our shots would aim to complement the narration. The camera would often provide the 'narrative'. To illustrate this, here is the script of one short sequence from the episode on skyscrapers, where the camera tracks in wide shot and close-up are devised in answer to the words against a further commentary provided by Carl Davis' music, which combines the sacred and the profane to underscore the contradictions implicit in Woolworth's sumptuous 'cathedral of commerce.'[8]

On Screen: Exterior Boom down/track forward through archway to reveal Woolworth Building.
Narration: In 1913 Cass Gilbert designed what is arguably the first fully resolved skyscraper, the Woolworth Building. Seven hundred and ninety-two feet high. It was a cathedral of commerce.
On Screen: Ext. wipe from traffic to low angle decorated entrance.
Narration: Only the Eiffel Tower was taller, yet where the Paris monument was all structural expression, the Woolworth Building revelled in the art of architecture.
On Screen: Int. tilt down to elevator ornamentation to Robert Stern speaking.
Narration: Boom up crane wide shot Lobby. Music: Woolworth theme composed by Carl Davis. In keeping with the theme of a cathedral of commerce, Gilbert designed the lobby as a great double-height church nave. Visitors would sweep into the building from Broadway, past confessional-like elevator booths which would take them to the tower high above.
On Screen: Track down medium shot from ceiling to bring into frame, revealing decorated cornices with vaults beyond. Track up mural to

The futuristic, nightmarish scenes of Metropolis, *1926*

reveal angel holding banner of 'commerce'.
Narration: The Woolworth Building was a cathedral. The walls were covered in marble, the cornices encrusted with gold leaf. The vaults above the nave were inlaid with millions of glass mosaic tiles. The galleries suspended above the transept were decorated with murals. They honoured the prophets appropriate to Woolworth's cathedral.
On Screen: Pivot close-up around carved portrait of Frank W Woolworth on bracket.
Narration: The carved brackets were medieval caricatures of the men responsible for the building.
On Screen: Focus pull to close-up Woolworth's hands fingering coins.
Narration: Frank W Woolworth counts the coins that paid for his tower. He had made his fortune as the king of the five-and-dime store and could afford to scoff at his bankers when they refused to finance his dream. Woolworth paid for the building in cash. Thirteen million dollars' worth of nickels and dimes.

The sequence continues with an exploration of this cathedral of contradictions with its 'unchurchlike' stairs. It ends with the carved gargoyle-like caricature of the architect, grasping his

tower, as a matched shot takes us into the sky to look down on the real Woolworth Building in all its shining glory, a proud white tower in the context of downtown Manhattan.

In the final analysis, film and television are primarily expected to tell stories. Audiences (or 'vidiences') want to be engaged by some form of narrative. Architecture as a subject is likely to spell box office poison to ratings-conscious executives. But one simply has to establish a new angle, however obtuse this may seem to them. Along with automobiles, buildings are our most important context, whether it is the 'overcoat' of a home, the consumer opportunity of a hypermarket, the public processional of the theatre or concert hall, or even the primal therapy of the sports stadium. On the other hand, the high percentage of lamentably bad buildings erected since the last World War, together with near universally poor urban planning, may have turned an entire generation off the importance of architecture to our daily lives. Could the vandals and graffiti artists of our inner cities be really architectural critics in despair? Once audiences make these connections with their own lives and experience, architecture will find its 'vidience'.

Notes

1 Peter Bogdanovich, *Pieces of Time*, New York, Arbor House/Esquire, 1973.

2 Donald Albrecht, *Designing Dreams: Modern Architecture in the Movies*, New York, Harper & Row and The Museum of Modern Art, 1986.

3 Raymond Durgnat, *Films and Feelings: Architecture in, and of, the Movies*, Cambridge, Mass., The MIT Press, 1967.

4 Nicholas Ray, 'My affection for CinemaScope initially was my affection for the horizontal line as I learned it from having been apprenticed to an architect who was someone named Frank Lloyd Wright.' Quoted in Eric Sherman for the American Film Institute, *Directing the Film: Film Directors on Their Art*, Boston, Little, Brown, 1976, p 128.

5 Kenneth Clark, *Civilisation: A Personal View*, New York, Harper & Row, 1969.

6 Vincent Scully, *Architecture: The Natural and the Manmade*, New York, Harvill/HarperCollins, 1991.

7 Vincent Scully, *American Architecture and Urbanisation*, New York, Praeger, 1969, p 257. 'Since civilization is based largely upon the capacity of human beings to remember, the architect builds physical history.'

8 'Pride of Place: Building the American Dream' (1986). Episode 7, *Proud Towers*, directed by Murray Grigor, Malone Gill Productions for Mobil, South Carolina Educational Television/PBS.

Still from Metropolis, *1926*

ANDREW BENJAMIN
AT HOME WITH REPLICANTS
The Architecture of Blade Runner

Where is the future? How will it be built? One way of taking up these questions would be to follow the presentation of the architectural within films that seek to project the future. The co-presence of the two – the architectural within film – brings two interrelated constraints into play. The first pertains to film; to its being a medium of representation. In this instance it will be the medium itself that works to constrain. Secondly, there will be the constraint of function. Even though the architecture of the future may differ, it will have to function as architecture. Even allowing for changes within it, difference will still be mediated by the retention of function. While this is clear that function is more complex than any idealisation of its presence will allow, what is of overall significance here is that the copresence of these constraints marks the necessity of relation. In being necessary it will have to be thought. The primordality of relation means that what will remain as an 'ineliminable' part of any built future is its being architecture. Equally, taking film, at least initially, as a medium of representation will mean that the images presented within it will need to be located within a visual field. Allowing for the fact that the nature of the image may need to be reconsidered, if not reassessed, film will, nonetheless, always have to represent.

What has been identified here as constraints may seem trivial. All they are asserting is that architecture must retain its specificity and that film must work with – and within – representation. And yet despite the apparently obvious nature of these assertions their importance lies in what they identify. In the case of both, their possibility lies in the necessity of a connection to the present. As such, both bring with them the importance and centrality of time. In the case of architecture the difficulty of thinking its future does not lie in a lack of imagination or capacity for futural projection, it is rather that the future and therefore its being thought will always need to be undertaken in relation to the present and, furthermore, to be seen as a condition of the present. Thus, the question of the future can always be reworked in terms of the possibility of another thinking. In the case of science fiction films, the challenge that arises with them is the extent to which what they are offering either in terms of film or, in this instance, of architecture amounts to that other possibility. Alterity here will always be different from projected utopias. On this account, the possibility of a pure utopia, a place outside of all relation, is an impossibility.

Before pursuing the interplay of film and architecture in *Blade Runner* – an interplay always conditioned by the work of constraint – a third element needs to be introduced. The presence of the body – the body within the architectural body as well as within the body of the film – will need to be taken up. Not only is the body implicated in the architectural by figuring, historically, as an important metaphor or analogy for the architectural, the move away from the physical human body towards the 'replicant', or more radically towards the cyborg, positions and holds the body in another form. It is reformed and maintained. The question hinges on what it is that is being maintained and how the analogy between architecture and body is structured by this change. It may be that other bodies will have been possible once the body – the possible other body – has to bear a relation to the present. Relation here is the site of critique; it is moreover critique's condition of possibility.

Los Angeles, November 2019, is the announced setting of Ridley Scott's *Blade Runner*. Here, the immediate problem is the presence on earth of Nexus 6 replicants. This advanced form of robot had been involved in mutinies in the 'Off World'. As a consequence, all replicants that manage to get back to earth are to be hunted down and then 'retired'. *Blade Runner* was the name given to those whose job it was to effect the retirement. The film's chronological setting, its urban location and the presence of replicants brings history (here the future), architecture (Los Angeles and the urban environment) and the body (eg the necessity to distinguish between replicant and human) into connection. Rather than taking this film either as programmatic or as having an exemplary status here its importance is that what it allows is a way of tracing a specific formation of these three elements. The importance of that formation is that it provides a way of thinking about the opening questions. Where is the future? How will it be built?

As the replicant is more or less indistinguishable from the human, special tests are needed in order to establish their identity. In the case of the Nexus 6, their capacity to develop more advanced emotional responses than the previous generation of replicants made their identification even more difficult and therefore correspondingly even more urgent. The test devised by Deckard involves observing pupil dilation during a detailed questioning. Replicants will in the end identify themselves by the inability to show the same level of immediate emotional response to certain questions. Within the structure of the film the presence of the replicant allows for a general questioning of the guarantees of identity. When Deckard and Rachael first meet, and before he is aware that she is a replicant, she asks Deckard whether he has 'ever retired a human by mistake?' At a later stage when she confronts him with her past – a past that in the process is truly identified as fiction – she pointedly inquires if he himself has taken his own test. In others words, the film by introducing and maintaining the possibility that Deckard may be a replicant heightens the already ambiguous replicant-human relation.

The level of gene technology that produced the 'skin jobs' is not just used with humans it is also deployed in the recreation of other animals. A trip through a market reveals snakes and ostriches among others. The owl at Tyrell headquarters is a replicant. There is an important level of instability that is introduced and reintroduced by the presence of these animals. It is interesting to note that this is brought about not through the use of hard technology but through work with genes. DNA manipulation has enabled the replicant to be produced. Here, the prosthetic is for the most part absent. Moreover, the use of drugs and virtual reality that complicates the constructed space in which, for example, Marva the main character in Pat Cadigan's *Fools* finds herself, is also absent. With this work the question of subjectivity is played out in terms of the human and the human's own creation. What is absent is the possible reworking and reposition of subject positions. It is this precise sense that the replicant can be distinguished from the cyborg. Donna Harrawy's own description of the cyborg is worth recalling.

> The cyborg is resolutely committed to partiality, irony, intimacy, innocence. No longer structured by the polarity of public and private, the cyborg defines a technological polis based partly on a revolution of social relations in the *oikos*, the household. Nature and culture can no longer be the resources for appropriation or incorporation by the other.

What does the cyborg offer? The answer to this question lies in the reference to the 'household'. The question is what force can the evocation of such a house hold? Its place will be problematic.

The architecture as well as interior design within *Blade Runner* is more straightforward. The police station to which Deckard is taken has an entrance area reminiscent of large rail stations – places in the American context which are already marked by a certain redundancy – while within the office the filing cabinets are wooden. The desk is conventional. The presence of fans indicates the absence or failure of air conditioning. Here, technology is only partly at work. The office indicates a continuity with a certain image of the present. On the other hand, the cars used by the police do not maintain the same level of continuity. They are technology at a very sophisticated level, or rather they are machines at a very sophisticated level. Technology is always used as a servant for the human. The potentially interactive space of man and machine only exists within a genetic context. Moreover, it is because the relationship between human and machine is located in opposition that the replicant is able to pose such a threat and more significantly why the architecture within the film has to enact a series of almost predictable conventions. What marks out the futural dimensions of the buildings?

Deckard's apartment is standard. It is not as though it enacts a yet-to-be determined structure of domesticity. It would be a perfect home for Rachael were she not a replicant. On one level what makes it seem unfair that they have to flee is that as a domestic setting it is ideal. And yet on another it could not be ideal as it is an architecture that could not house the consequences of her having been accepted. Accepting the replicant may demand another architecture. As a work of architecture, his apartment's only concession to the future – and here would be a putative concession – is the voice activated lift and the location of his apartment on the 97th floor. Although it introduces a further element of instability into the film there is the strong suggestion that the majority of the population have left and now inhabit the 'Off World'. Immigrant communities, corporate headquarters, elements of government and those who work within them seem to be all that has remained. And yet why this works to open up the question of the architecture of the other world (in the end this question is otiose) is because there is no need to think that the relationship between human and technology – be that technology machine or gene based – would be any different.

The Tyrell headquarters seems to be modelled on a Mayan temple. Internally, its architecture and design is eclectic. A visionary future is held at bay by size. As with the elevation of Deckard's apartment, here the only concession to the future – albeit an imagined future – is enormity. Conversely, other architectural possibilities are provided by the transformation of the given; however, the transformation in question is decay. What comes to be juxtaposed within the cosmopolitan urban fabric is decay – the continuity rather than the teleology of decay – and the modern vast. The replicant is seen as a threat within this context. It is at this point that the constraint governing both architecture and film needs to be reintroduced.

What characterises the replicant is its filmic possibility. Rachael, Pris, Zhora are ostensibly human. They are not stylised machines. In the case of Roy, his poignant claim that he has seen and experienced more than any human almost makes him more human than the humans. It is as though he has lived at the very edge of human existence. Indeed, his death – he dies by simply running out of life – seems the most quintessentially human aspiration for death. Neither killed nor fatally ill his life just runs out at the appointed time. At that moment he shows himself to be what the replicant had always been, namely an other who was never absolutely other. Robots, androids, the dolls populating JF Skinner's apartment – even the machine with skin – would always be purely other. Acts of differentiation would be straightforward. Differences would proliferate and insist. The body of the replicant does not allow for complete differentiation. They are both part of the set-up while not being part

of it. They become, therefore, a mediating moment. Their filmed presence allows them to be the same but only in the moment of their differentiation. Equally that presence allows them to be different by presenting them as the same. As body and as the analogue for architecture they are both at home and not at home.

The replicant works through the opposition of same and other by turning that opposition into an identity by incorporating it. As such, the architectural aesthetic within *Blade Runner* that posits an otherness that is only explicable in terms of decay and size has done no more than heighten possibilities already present in contemporary urban life. The disruptive possibility of a relation with a replicant arises because of the recognition of the actuality of alterity. This can be worked through both in relation to the replicant itself or in terms of a necessary concession about the already divided nature of self. The architecture of the film cannot provide an architecture for replicants. A refusal – articulated within a banalised conception of architectural otherness – leaves open the question of what it would mean to be at home with replicants. Answering it must work through the analogy between architecture and body; this time, however, taking the replicant's body as the point of departure. Only by starting with replicants will it be possible to house cyborgs.

Deckard (Harrison Ford) among the decayed, urban landscape of Los Angeles, in the year 2019

NIKOS GEORGIADIS
ARCHITECTURAL EXPERIENCE AS DISCOURSE OF THE (UN)FILMED

The relationship between film and architecture today appears to be no longer that of a mutual correspondence.[1] Urban/architectural reality seems uninspiring as filmic material while its everyday experience is progressing in a way which devaluates and trivialises cinematic imagery. What might we learn from such a distantiation? Could this be a moment of critique between the two or is it just another case of discursive alienation? Moreover, while film discourse as *directing visuality* maximises the visual paradigm, questions of representation, reality, and their mutual transference are reintroduced.

This paper meets architecture 'as discourse' through another discursive experience (the film); it meets it not in a represented form but as a paradox of film discourse arising from the side of the filmable object and thus as potential critique to the film. So questions such as that of the 'filmability of architecture' are reversed into a questioning of the degree of awareness and embedding of the architectural dimension in the process of filmmaking. Also, architectural experience takes the opportunity to be rediscovered not positively – as film image vocabulary – but in terms of real spatial processes whose complexity and instrumentality architects, no matter how intuitively, are already familiar with, and to the extent that such processes can appear as *operational* difficulties within film.

Filmic difficulties have been discussed in terms of the filmability of 'vision' and the 'image of the woman' as political issues in cinema; both seemed impossible, being simultaneously preoccupations of the filming consciousness and sought after radical forms on the side of the filmed object (ie the subject both as spectator and as caught up in the actual field of his visual mastery, the image of the woman both as preconceived within representation and phallic reference and as a quested 'pre-representational' visual alternative).[2] However, it can be suggested that the difficulty here was how to break away from the *scenariocentric, camera/image bipolar structure*. Such a difficulty was intensified by the uncritical use of Lacanian psychoanalysis made on the basis of a discursive adaptation of basic concepts such as those of the Imaginary or the Real. Within the context of cinema these concepts appeared to justify

either the camera's discursive visual certainty as Imaginary uninterrupted plenitude on behalf of the *viewer*, or its uncertainty (countervisuality) on behalf of the *viewed*[3] or *viewing back image*;[4] whereas the hunting of 'alternative visual forms' positivised concepts like the Unconscious and Desire in terms of radical imagery (always specific to the camera consciousness), which was dangerously appropriable by the repressive agencies those images were meant to criticise.[5] The psychoanalytic analogy seemed to disqualify the aspects of *acting* and *transference* specific to the sensory field of the film (essential to psychoanalysis too), since it regarded the subjects of both psychoanalytic and filmic experience as coincidental, and assumed an automatic transference of the audience onto either the viewer or the image (eg the character or object as gaze) – two positions firmly enclosed within the scenario-guided camera consciousness (identifying or counter-identifying with it, respectively). A related new realism arose in political filmmaking assuming a spontaneous transference to the character's image, incarnating a self-critical, conflictual or 'analytic' consciousness pre-set by the scenario and its appointed imagery; while reducing reality to nothing more than a supplier of images and film experience into a mere simulation of literature.[6] Cinema appeared as an absurd purveyor of psychoanalytic material automatically corresponding with the psychic structure and often reaching the status of an alternative psychoanalytic theory; whereas psychoanalytic concepts, detached from their original context, began to acquire peculiar philosophical dimensions: either as a negative transcendentalism of the image (Real; a blend of the psychotic and the Foucauldian subject) or as unproblematic autonomous psychic instances (Imaginary).[7]

As regards *filmic difficulties*, the question never answered was how these instances might become areas of re-theorisation and potential instrumentation (a 'positive solution') on the level of the discourse of the object-to-film as constitutive of the filmic site and critical of the camera/image conduct. The attack on the camera's visual idealism is inadequate in terms of a mere acknowledgement of the nonreal status of the filmed object[8] and also in terms of transcendentalising its counterpart – the image. If there is a 'reality residue' somewhere in film discourse, this should arise as a critical externality enabling proper relations of transference – through performance. What could introduce psychoanalysis here, then, is not a 'Subject analogy' of the viewer or the viewed, but the urge for a *transverse subjectivity* via the real film-work, which would condition the transference of the audience into the political film and the question it raises. This paper adds a further filmic difficulty to those mentioned above: that of urban/architectural experience cutting across the camera-register and its filmable object. This is placed as a response to the scenariocentric camera/image discourse, the psychoanalytic analogy and, moreover, as a symptomatic response to the issues discussed on the question of the 'filmability of the city' on the occasion of a film-week in Athens from which the visual material was collected (see note 1).

During this event, the 'image of Athens' was raised as a question of political significance with regard to both film and architecture. Athens was regarded as a 'lost image' in two senses, as uninspiring to filmmaking and as quested through films. So, urban experience appeared both as a preoccupation of the camera's conduct[9] and as a sought after critical image – a potential model for architectural design. In criticising today's city/architecture as being poor in image and unavailing of filmable material, filmmakers' views sounded architecturally naive and literary, whereas cinema was presented as more architecturally interesting than architecture itself. All films shown were meant to represent urban experience in its sociocultural, historical, etc, dimension. If 'progressive' filmmaking mentioned the city as (an inspiring) part of the filmic agency, in the discussion which followed among architects the design of the 'progressive' city was sought in terms of its imageability. In both cases, architecture was held firmly within the scenario/camera bind, as a supplier and instigator of images or as a filmicly processed image. The above view was epitomised by a film (metafilm), *Athens, Seeking the Lost City*,[10] produced for the occasion made up of extracts from films, mainly city-shoots. In its attempt to give a categorical representation of the city, the film over-relied on montage, eventually homogenising spatial experience and depoliticising the image of the city, cutting it off from its original position in those films. A voice-over narration connecting a mosaic of city profiles was added to maintain minimal identification of the viewer with the camera, appearing as a conventional plot-gesture in the film discourse's defence *vis-à-vis* the filmed object; and yet montage as cut-up visuality already indicates a *city metaphor* (the film as city – urban fragmented space and the interchange-

ability of episodes serving as a metaphor for montage). The 'film' was therefore useful in a contrary (to its director's intentions) way, since in handling urban space both as embedded in the flâneuring/montaging camera (see note 9) and as (re-proposed) imagery, the film conduct, as such, was trivialised into a loose and descriptive literary narrative.

The resistance to the filming agency resets the problem of the city's filmability as a question of politics of spatial experience. In what follows we attempt to highlight such a filmic impossibility, as a locus of film critique and encounter with architecture. The concept of the *acting-over image* will thus be pursued in the field of architectural experience – as (un)filmed object, critical to the scenario-guided, camera/image consciousness (specific to the directing agent or the directed image). This in turn will invite the psychoanalytic concept of the *Imaginary*, as a formative and dialectical instance for subjectivity, to enable a critical understanding of the image across film and architecture beyond the visual/countervisual paradigm. The scenes selected from three Greek films[11] exemplify spatial experience symptomatically not only to the film event but also to the directing intentions of the films they were taken from. They introduce the politics of the *domestic object*, the *urban experience* and the *landscape/environment* insofar as these 'neutral' settings (serving the character, the episode and the scenario, respectively) can, via acting, transfer the audience to the world of intentional space.

The Object Versus the Character

'Mr Runabout' (*'Papatrehas'*) or *The Odd-Job Man* is a film about a caretaker of a modern multidwelling building in Athens. His background is trivial, he seems to have no social identity, while his actual role in the building exceeds that of mere caretaker since he does all sorts of odd jobs. This particular scene shows him struggling, in a classic slapstick manner, with an increasing number of domestic objects handed to him by residents for errands. A rope, a plant, a cage containing two birds, a suit for cleaning, a bucket of water, all these he grabs with his hands, then with his teeth, even before he is told what to do with them, carrying them around and eventually falling over. In a later sequence he is meddling with the actual parts of the building using his body in a quite unorthodox way, often crashing onto the staircase, the doors, or the floor. Finally, he gets onto the roof from which he falls, but, held by the washing line, he bounces down the facade of the building, eventually reaching street level from where he is ready to begin over again. All this happens in an *incidental* (rather than accidental) manner, disclosing a sense of overstatement of realness

Stills from Mr Runabout, 1966, *('Papatrehas')*

27

rather than disturbances of representation from which the scene appears to be operating at a distance. Furthermore, it is this sense which entitles us to regard the *actor as role*, to identify with the real actor rather than with the role he plays (notably, this comic film actor almost always plays using his 'real' name).

The scene opens up the acting/performing body onto a reality excess, affording a multiple re-relating with a plethora of already customised domestic objects involving the building itself. The caretaker operates *within the positive* world of objects and pragmatics; he is in the homely, (re)identifying with fragments of people's primary narcissism (recurring as care for the object), which he reshuffles and overstates. His concern is not significations but their very referent, the real object, with which he introduces a second imaginary instance. The city for him is a natural extension of the domestic world, having no mystery, appearing as an endless articulation of already familiarised objects which extend from the 'domestic' to the 'urban', even to the outskirts; and he is equally attracted by all of them. He introduces a bearable (comic) lightness of presences (the 'already being'), caught up in domestication processes, outside symbolic or pre-symbolic relationships. Symbolic communication is neither disturbed by nor asymptotic to his position; it is, rather, under quest. The objects he holds together across space are infinite, while his hyperacting body 're-presentifies' them, *realising once more their real presence*. Close to Tati's style (eg in *Mon Oncle*), objects, signification-wise, appear shallow and trivial, they 'virtually' mean nothing, their original discursive significance having become unimportant, eliminated even. The scene remodifies the camera's conduct, as the visual field becomes overcrowded with objects whose interaction within the actors' orbit cancels any sense of depth, of front or background. Here, an antimontage effect occurs whereby objectal reality 'montages back' reasoning visuality specific to the significations of each one of these objects. A similar sense of shallowness in terms of symbolic meaning or message-emitting develops throughout the film. An anti-realist process comes into play with a total absence of dramatisation,[12] a subjectless process, encouraging a peculiar empathisation between the spectator and these animated fragments of pure presence. The body is not vulnerable even though it crashes into everything; it rather proposes an *odd-job activism* whose multi-serving of discourses cancels their differences. Here 'anything can happen' in terms of an endless possibility of object-relating; the spectator will not be surprised by any dismantling of significations but, instead, will find relief in and enjoy this unusual trivialisation of them.

The Street Versus the Episode

Laterna, Poverty and Pride is a film about two travelling 'laterna' (street-organ) players. Their familiarisation with the city allows them not a marginal position but social recognition and respect. In one episode (not central to the film) we see them falling victims to the invasion of cars in the streets of Athens. They are trapped in the middle of a narrow crossroads with cars coming towards them from all directions. Although frozen in the middle, they are not actually obstructing the traffic since traffic itself has become impossible, with cars screeching to a halt facing one another.

It is the logic of the already customised space of the streets, as activated in the scene, that rescues them, protecting them not only from the tooting cars but also from their recurrence into the symbolic, ie from becoming a nostalgic remnant of a fading 'street' culture; furthermore, it saves them from a street fight. The scene can be said to rescue subjectivity in the form of reality-discourse and at the cost of the loss of the symbolic dimension. There appears an impossible *place symptomatic* to the Dasein of the modern 'city', hystericising its well-being; an Other city whose 'form' not only does not follow its function but makes function itself appear as an obsolete form. Urban space returns as repressed and repositions the two players not in terms of an impotent cultural residue *vis-à-vis* modernisation, but by justifying them in the streets as part of a fully instrumental spatial experience, as the traffic, now a useless signification, freezes in the middle of the street.

By enacting space, the scene shifts the episode outside any realist narrative (hence the humour) which, by contrast, a discursive antithesis between the 'old' and 'new' urban culture could easily fall into. A sense of disrationality is effected as urban experience operates at a distance from the symbolic logic it is meant to serve; from neutrally serving the traffic, the street now becomes (a not uncanny but) an *inconveniently hyperserving device*, excessively realising its 'task'. In an unusual psychoanalytic manner, we witness the realisation of a fundamental discordance between the imaginary (the expected) of the modern street function (ie quick car access), and the real (ie the traffic jam and impossibility of motion). Urban space affords more than one – antithetical to one another – expression of the same signification which it is supposed to serve. It thus qualifies the spectator's interest as a subjectivity peculiar to the sociocultural dimension. The modern city is criticised by the spatial structure of the street (the very referent of the urban episode), which not only diffuses the episode's signifying aspect within the film but its 'realness' also deducts it from the very signifying plane of the scenario,

Slapstick behaviour from Mr Runabout

introducing a state of *non-episode* before the camera (whose plot-minded task is meant to be that of reporting, directing and effecting the episode and then montaging it with others). Here is a 'nothing happened' situation, hence nothing to film. Put another way, 'anything can happen in the streets', not as an unpredictable accidentality but as a spatial *provision* as well as *forgetting* of the signifying event, or, again, as a possible de-intentionalisation of the symbolic aspect of the episode, and thus de-memorisation of the urban experience, whereby spectator and citizen find relief.

Both the caretaker and the street-organ players point at a psychological state different from that of a contemporary *flâneur*,[13] namely a 'no-body' lost in the crowd who manoeuvres and finds his way around things; the man on the street who, individually, rationalises (and familiarises with) the 'negative' side of the city which eventually becomes his symbolic home. In opposition to that, here is a *spatial (every)-body*,[14] who does not 'appropriate' architectural or urban experience (or use the former as metaphor for the latter) since he is in it already, enfiguring our constant, immediate experience with space extending from domestic objects to the city itself, as he easily reidentifies with them, putting in question their reason. He does not 'know' the city, but he becomes the city and the objects, initiating a dialectic on their behalf. In that respect, the city does not surprise but concern him, and rather surprises us insofar as we insist on visualising our relationship with it. He is not an existentialist, he does not *positivise negativity*; he is, rather, *in the positive*, not as objectified figure but as *enfigured object*. He is no-character, not because he negates the character aspect and his reason of existence but because he sustains and affords the experience of loss of character in its symbolic dimension, capable of mapping the lack of reason. He is not a nostalgic figure, but stands critically to the historicised, symbolic present. He has no origin as he can afford to redefine it – origin for him is constantly under quest not under threat. He does not search for 'real' experiences but is already 'grown up' in reality and, rather, architecturally mature.

The Landscape Versus the Scenario
Eudokia is a film that is highly aware of the instrumental value of space/reality (*vis-à-vis* the camera conduct) and also the disadvantages any plot complexity might entail for the critical rigour of the film. The story is simple and the spectator familiarises with it within the first few minutes. It looks as if the rest of the film highlights the real objectal world to which the story refers. The story develops in the years of the military coup, between a prostitute (Eudokia)

and a sergeant (George) in military service in a barracks outside Athens. They fall in love and get married, but their relationship is doomed to fail as Eudokia cannot escape her background and George, after finishing his service, loses all social pride by being poor, out of work, and humiliated by his wife's reputation.

Sociocultural categories like those of 'the prostitute', 'the pimp', 'the soldier', 'relatives', 'friends', are treated as objectified, referentless significations projected onto hard but liveable landscapes, in a style reminiscent of Pasolini's *Medea* and *Oedipus Rex*. *Eudokia* then landscapes all settings and the characters themselves, as power, law, sexuality, are parcelled as objectal states of significations, not specific to characters but rather exchanged and circulating among subject-referents. A series of spaces arises, including home interiors, front yards, neighbourhood streets, taverns, the beach, the landscape outside the town, the barracks, the brothel etc; all are spaces in use, bearing traces of their previous users, anti-Dasein (but not uncanny)[15] and *inconvenient spaces not because they are unhomely or inhuman but because they are overtly human* in offering accommodation to both the real and the imaginary instantiations of those signifying discourses they are supposed to accommodate and serve.[16] *Landscape* here stands for that spatial quality, which always affords a sense of Otherness and inappropriability because of the very event of its customisation, the latter being its precondition. It is inconvenient because of its use and in the course of it. Unlike Antonioni's idealised negative or abandoned landscapes, this is not an empty space, open to signification, neither a shapeless, mythical one, nor an 'unfolding space of intensity'; it is neither friendly, nor hostile, nor intriguing, but real space in which no marks of subjectivity are to be found other than pure presences of symbolic wholes (lost and found), enabling processes of initiation, anticipation and exposure of significations by their own referents.[17] Landscape, as a technique figuring in the film, proposes spaces which collocate both experiences of 'how things really *are*' and 'how they *should be*' in *realising a given symbolic structure* (be it the story, episode or character), spaces which encourage and sustain such a distinction between these two symbolic poles, spaces of real copresence of 'reality' and 'hope', of minimal fulfilment and great expectations.

The *moving-landscape scene* perhaps best exemplifies the operational dimension of space. George takes a day absent without leave to meet Eudokia and they end up on a hill just outside the city. She jumps on a swing hanging from a tree, as he on the ground pushes her controlling the movement; the landscape appears as a still

Scene from Laterna, Poverty and Pride, 1955

background to the swinging Eudokia and pushing George as the camera shoots the two. He then jumps on the swing; the camera, too, jumps on the swing, not to follow but to coincide with his movement. As the two entwined bodies disappear, the visual field radically changes since camera and audience are placed in the actual position of the actors, identifying with them in the course of their swinging, missing presence. What we see on the screen is a moving landscape from the ground to the sky and back. The only trace of the two lovers on the screen is Eudokia's loud, orgasmic laughter covering the whole sequence. Subsequently, they reappear on the screen in a silent shot where he, standing, stares at the sunset, while she is still oscillating. He proposes marriage; she replies: 'so soon? . . . OK, done!' (an unfortunate marriage which seems to integrate the whole scenario). What we actually see on the screen is not a 'to-and-fro' oscillation of the two characters or the camera (these are just thought-forms in our minds); on the contrary, we are introduced into the real film experience of a moving landscape enrhythmed by the swing, repeating and referring to itself, a self-polarised movement between the earthground and the sky, the bushes and the trees, 'close' and 'far', yet between 'nature' and the city appearing far away. The landscape no longer makes itself available to the camera's intentions; its movement offers a phenomenological condition on the screen, overtaking viewing consciousness.

Before George and the camera jump on the swing, the spectator (watching the episode progressing before her/him) identifies with the camera's plot-guided viewing consciousness directing the scene ('to see Eudokia'), within pre-assumed male/female enrolments and imagery associated with the city/state law, the locus of male sexuality (and visuality) and Oedipal relations. Then the landscape sequence shifts the spectator onto the position of the filmed object, effecting an unfilmic instance within the film by bringing together, in an analytic manner, *visuality, the image of the woman* and *the city*, perhaps cinema's most indispensable objects to be filmed – a common a priori for cinematic significations. The spectator can no longer identify either with the camera's visual/countervisual certainty, or with the pre-assumed sexual imagery, or with the city/state's built and territorial form, since they are all missing from the field of vision; what is precisely missing are these conceptual images 'assumed' by the filming consciousness (be it expressive of the director's intentions or the viewer's expectations). What drops as a useless object is the literary, thought-form, Cartesian certainty, ie the scenario conduct (as instructing the camera, enroling desire and sexuality, rationalising and

legislating space). Now, what is instead subjectified is the formerly filmable object activating the actual referents of those significations, namely the visual field (formerly the background setting), sexual course and difference, and the landscape (the city's left-over 'free space').

Firstly, the visual/countervisual paradigm, specific to the director or spectator, fails. The camera's jump onto the swing introduces an unvisual instance within visuality which shifts subjectivity outside ocular (counter- or multi-ocular) vicissitudes, familiarising us with real *relations of exposure* and *enfigured vision* (formerly the 'natural' counterpart of visuality). There is nothing to see, nothing to see you either; the only thing appearing on the screen is an agitated field (in front of which the directing camera becomes still and unviewing), as the referent of visual signification is activated specularly to the viewing intentions, via and against the movement of the viewing consciousness, establishing subjectivity in a field of inverted visuality.[18] Such an anti-voyeuristic experience is amplified by the unfulfilled urge of the audience to see the lovemaking couple on the swing as Eudokia's screaming gets louder. Voyeurism becomes an impotent imagination, literary in form, residing in the audience's heads, as any attempt for identification with the camera conduct leads us to a pure referentless 'thinking' position; the camera specifies the locus of a still, male, reasoning but blind visuality, exposed to the discourse of the filmed field.

Secondly, the woman's presence is signified only by her orgasmic laughs, indicating a locus of sexuality that is not self-referential but *intercursive* and critical. Avoiding any image-positivisation, as identification or counter-identification with the real phallic object, the imageless seat of the woman enables, in the field of enacted vision, an analytic situation as regards the phallic conduct confronting it as historical-material signification (rather than as pure concept or transcendental object); it deducts from it (via film technique and not as visually represented by the film image)[19] its sexual imagery altogether, while reintroducing it as an obsolete, symbolic (Oedipal) law. The woman, insofar as her image is part of such a conduct, is deleted from the visual field and, insofar as she is a locus of Otherness and transference, is traced as intercursive orgasmic laughter. *The woman as locus rather than as image*, points at a potential epistemological position, an *encore*-discourse of having and exposing reason rather than of being it.[20] Visuality/blindness, as long as they are expressive of the two ends of the formation of symbolic law (primary narcissism and castration), seem not to concern such a position; the woman does

The moving landscape scene from Eudokia, 1971

not look but allocates the look in a gesture beyond the menacing gaze.[21]

Thirdly, the city fades at the bottom of the hill where the swing-play progresses, giving way to an overwhelming activation of the 'countryside' (formerly neutralised, subservient to the city's ongoing expansion). The city reappears in its repressed dimension – the landscape – not as a natural 'countryside' but a return of that spatial quality which the law of the city/state had appropriated and foreclosed as an unmediated necessity. The procedural landscape challenges us (as subjects to the symbolic law) for an infinite repositioning from 'here' to 'there' and back again, an opening within Dasein itself, offering instances of *intentionalised space*. As in the drama of Antigone, the city, in its symbolic (sociocultural, etc) dimension is criticised as a whole, *outside* its walls, its territory-marks, on a plane of a spatial pulsating permanency persisting in the symbolic.[22] From there, one becomes witness to the self-indulging and self-cancelling character of its symbolic structures (eg the law of the state and the army).

The Acting-Over Body

The actor returns as a major (so far foreclosed) film subjectivity within and against the scenario-centric camera/image bind. The acting body sustains the *transference* of the spectator as identifying with the camera/image filming agent onto the actual site of the film. It sustains not a unification but a split between these two positions, exposes the literary register of the visual (and sexual) self-consciousness and treats it as an object; whereas it organises, via the film, a discourse on the side of customised space. The acting body does not play or express the given symbolic part, rather (re)realises it, affording a sense of reality which devirtualises the neo-realist structure of the three scripts. The *actor's realism* arises from the filmed object *un-reflectedly*, as regards the scenario-conduct; s/he is not an objectified subjectivity, but subjectifies inanimate objects, becoming her/himself a symbolicless intentionality.[23] The actor points to a non-subjectivity but, then again, to a state of affairs *like* subjectivity. By enfiguring reality, ie what visual/counter-visual consciousness referentialises as worth seeing, the body becomes uncontrollable, disobeying the viewing conduct and introducing extra-scenario and extra-visual instances. Thus, *performance* and 'improvisation' reappear in a negative dimension and constitute a major *directing* authority in the film. Acting is sustained beyond the actor's screen presence whose symbolic dimension (specific to the character, episode, scenario, the main representation-sources of the object, the city and the environment) is criticised accordingly in the three scenes; the body, via an

excessive presence in motion constantly re-encountering domestic objects, unsignifies the character/person; then, in a state of *slow or frozen presence* over-familiarising with real urban space, falsifies the signifying episode; and, finally, highlighted in its visual *absence*, becoming an enfigured movement onto the procedural landscape, unbinds the scenario itself. The actor is not 'overacting' a given role, becoming her/himself a nonsubject;[24] rather, the body is *acting over* a given signification; and that precisely touches already familiar grounds in architectural experience. It treats reality in an unorthodox way by regarding it as an already accomplished process, and re-registering with it outside its signifying conduct. The body does not perform reality as might happen in theatre, but sustains performance on the level of reality.[25]

Spatial Experience

Acting thus takes sides with the film object/space, without suggesting any environmental/objectal consciousness or a negativity of a sublime or transcendental kind on the side of object-image;[26] rather, it renders this very object-image excessive and figurative.[27] In all scenes reality is handled not as unmediated – 'as it really is' – but as self-repeated.[28] The experience of *recustomisation of already customised space* (reality-experience in itself) is commonplace within architectural practice and seems to be ignored by advocates of the Real and aestheticised negativity, and by 'philosophisers' of architecture.[29] So is subjectivity which, either as a depersonalised human reinvolved in object-relations, or witnessing the trivialisation of its significations via use, or even experiencing itself within and against visuality, emerges through phenomena which, before any analysis, already constitute familiar experiences in architectural reality. The encounter with architecture and liveable space does not happen via dramatised metastatements of the negative, the Real and death, overloading the character, the episode, the scenario with intentions they might not have had in the first place.[30] It, instead, happens via the activation of the spatial sensory register, disclosing a sense of lightness (comic relief) and enjoyment,[31] transferring the audience into the unfilmable, which now becomes operational. Indeed, the advent of *reality-experience* specifies a filmic process operating as a kind of 'natural' setting-on-scene of the role, the episode and the scenario. Relations of visuality are inverted into *relations of exposure* over which film and architecture meet non-analogously: the exposed, formerly assumed as deintentionalised fact, now becomes an intentionality. The unfilmable 'films back' the film, treating its script the same way the film treated spatial experience. The phenom-

Stills from Eudokia

enology of customised space introduces the architectural dimension as an agitated and unreflected Dasein (an *idle reality* perhaps) which renders problematic any pictorial reductionism or essentialism, while the rigour of the congested image returns as a process of *image-inating* rather than an 'invaginating'/ pleated plasticity.[32] If a general comment is to be allowed here, cinema as 20th-century art does not seem justifiable in terms of a phenomenology of 'moving image'– moving inside the city as 'timing' visuality compressing and resignifying urban experience[33] – but should be seen as a form of a symptomatic return, within the world of visual arts, of spatial experience as the repressed faculty of image-processing of time and signification.

The Imaginary

On the psychoanalytic level, the excessive appearance of the image in the dimension of the real 'presentified' object entitles us to recognise the return of the Imaginary rather than the Real or any kind of object-metaphor.[34] A *pure, corporeal, Umwelt image* returns onto already virtualised reality, creating conditions of designification. In the first sequence, the Imaginary returns as a peculiar reintroducibility (re-imagisation) of an already accomplished structure; in the second as articulation, specific to the urban space, peculiar to the symbolic order; and, in the third, as a form of global imaginary – a negatively universal locality, and a peculiar locus of desire and loss.

In response to some early readings[35] some differences in the way in which the Imaginary appears might be listed: (a) it holds a symptomatic position in the film, binding an unfilmic signifying agency, operating as critical exteriority, thus inappropriate to justify a general film theory; (b) it is met as a state of affairs simulating subjectivity and operating in the area of the filmed object, and not as plenitude on the spectator's side justifying her/his identification with the camera whose symbolic dimension it thereby exposes and criticises; (c) in the scenariocentric camera/image discourse the Imaginary does not hold the status of an absent function but of an ultra-represented, foreclosed agency, always available to the camera's viewing intentions whose counterpart/image is but a visual 'positivisation' of the concept; and (d) it returns into and against the filmic certainty as a repressed, nonphilosophical discourse, both historically and politically valid, and not as an arbitrary metaphor.

Since the Imaginary returns as a function, not in progress but already accomplished, one can argue that psychoanalysis enters the discourse of these unfilmic instances in a position critical to any automatic identification between the psychoanalytic subject and the camera or the image (distinguishing between the making of subjectivity and the making of the film). Now, with those instances supportable by the 'experienceful' paradigm of architecture, a series of symptomatic affiliations among *the discourse of directing vision*, *psychoanalysis* and *architecture* could lead to further research.

What lies behind Parhassios' veil is, surely, neither Norman's murderous gaze (or his mother's skull) nor the cut-off genitals from Oshima's realm of senses. Rather, there lies the involuntary, light discourse of a series of truly unhappy Hegelian objects. And, behind such unhappiness, might well lie the intercursive laughter of Eudokia ('Eu-doxa') – 'well thought' and well protected from the tricks of visuality, well identifying with the pulsating landscape, which comes and goes as a reinviting return, an *encore*, one more chance for the stranded soldier/ spectator to jump on the swing and pass onto the side of the *real-ly* Other. Should he miss . . .

Notes

The conceptual framework of this paper relates to an academic research on architecture and psychoanalysis.

1 A major question raised during a film-week entitled 'Athens: Seeking the Lost City' held at the French Institute, Athens, 22-27 November 1993.

2 Questions formulated by Jacqueline Rose in 'The Imaginary' (1975) and 'The Cinematic Apparatus – Problems in Current Theory' (1980), in her collection of essays *Sexuality in the Field of Vision* (London: Verso, 1986), pp 166-97 and pp 198-213.

3 See J Rose's critique on Christian Metz's concept of 'Imaginary Signifier' (Christian Metz, *Psychoanalysis and Cinema* (London: Macmillan, 1983), in J Rose (1975), p 167).

4 An elaboration of the Lacanian *gaze* and the *Real* on the level of the film image can be found in some works on Hitchcock, eg Slavoj Zizek, 'In His Bold Gaze my Ruin is Writ Large' in S Zizek (ed), *Everything You Always Wanted to Know About Lacan . . .* (London: Verso, 1992 (a)), pp 247-63.

5 For a general discussion of these issues see Hal Foster (ed), *Vision and Visuality* (Washington: Bay Press, 1988), pp ix-xiv, and J Rose's 'Sexuality and Vision: Some Questions' in this publication, pp 115-126.

6 A Brechtian metaphor – S Freer's *My Beautiful Launderette* or I Julian's *Young Soul Rebels* can illustrate the point.

7 For the Imaginary, see C Metz (1983) (a view subsequently criticised in J Rose (1975)), and for the Real, see Slavoj Zizek, *Enjoy Your Symptom* (London: Routledge, 1992 (b)), pp 178-86.

8 J Rose (1975), p 195.

9 Reference was made to Wenders' analogy between film images and city streets, in relation to the binding necessity of the scenario. See Wim Wenders (a), *The Logic of Images* (London: Faber and Faber, 1991) and (b) 'The City: A Conversation', interview with Hans Kollhoff, *Quaderns d'Arquitectura i Urbanisme*, No 177, April/May/June 1989.

10 A film made by M Gastine and S Dracopoulos.

11 *Mr Runabout* or *Papatrehas* by E Thalassinos, the leading role played by T Veggos (1966); *Laterna, Poverty and Pride* by A Sakellarios (1955); *Eudokia* by A Damianos (1971).

12 The scene's unsensational character brings the actor close to the Untragic hero of Brecht's *epic theatre* but lies outside both realisms: Lukács' formalist/literary reality-consciousness amplifying the camera's mastery, and Brecht's consciousness of discursive conflict at the level of the image. See Bertolt Brecht 'Against Georg Lukács' in *Aesthetics and Politics* (London: NLB, 1977), pp 68-85; Walter Benjamin, 'What is Epic Theatre?' in *Understanding Brecht* (London: NLB, 1973 (b)), pp 1-25; and Colin Mac-Cabe, *Theoretical Essays: Film, Linguistics, Literature* (Manchester University Press, 1985), pp 33-80.

13 A vagabond figure watchfully observing the city in full possession of his individuality. See Walter Benjamin, *Charles Baudelaire* (London: NLB, 1973 (a)), pp 35-69.

14 This is neither a nomadic nor a vagabond figure; but affiliates with and somewhat expands the Blanchotian 'autrui' which designates a respected strangership (or guestship), yet fellowmanship – a disarmingly speechless sense of presence. See Maurice Blanchot, *The Infinite Conversation* (Minnesota University Press, 1993).

15 Here the spatial uncanny is taken as a notion related to the dedomesticated subject as coming from literature, psychology and philosophy, or as a metaphor for the 'unlivable modern condition'. See Anthony Vidler, *The Architectural Uncanny: Essays in the Modern Unhomely*, (MIT Press, 1992).

16 A similar handling of space can be seen in the Argentinian film *Last Images of the Shipwreck* by Eliseo Subiela.

17 A process somehow resembling the deciphering of hieroglyphics and dreams (Freud's *Übertragung*). See Jacques Lacan, *Book I: Freud's Papers on Technique*, 1953-54 (Cambridge University Press, 1988).

18 The elimination of the director/spectator viewing position by the very visual field which the camera takes for granted is excellently performed in the last sequences of Michael Powell's *Peeping Tom* whereby the *filmic* survives beyond the *filming* at the cost of directing visuality, which, before becoming redundant, passes via the position of acting in its own film as the killing director becomes the actor of his last film-image (killing him). This can be seen as the film's superiority in comparison with Hitchcock's *Psycho* which retains a firm directing/spectating consciousness which takes advantage of even the most 'disturbing' ima-gery,notably resolved within the highly explanatory progression of the scenario.

19 Here, the identification of the woman with reality in a manner meeting the film technique itself beyond mere visuality, should be distinguished from any identification with the Real as filmable gaze within the field of the film's visual representation. (An example of the latter can be found in Oshima's *In the Realm of the Senses* where the woman carries her lover's genitals around the town, identifying with and sublimating the real object (cut-off penis) – an example put forward by Mark Cousins at the Bataille symposium, Architectural Association, London, May 1991.)

20 See Jacques Lacan, *Ecrits – A Selection* (London: Tavistock, 1977), p 207, and *Encore* (Paris: Seuil, 1975).

21 A term which in Lacan has a metaphoric meaning but in Sartre stands as a positivisation of Negativity.See also Norman Bryson, 'The Gaze in the Expanded Field' in Foster (ed)(1988).

22 See also Jacques Lacan, *The Ethics of Psychoanalysis*, 1959-60 (London: Routledge, 1992), pp 270-82.

23 Within the Brechtian paradigm (W Benjamin (1973 (b)), pp 17-

23) and against it, the actor is an undramatic figure, a *sage*, but in a non-Platonic way. Gesturality or grimacing are not taken from the consciousness of today's reality (conflictual or not) and so are not necessarily *quotable* or familiar to the audience; they take their shape from what such a consciousness takes for granted as 'real' and sensual; a process also reminiscent of the surrealists' 'optical realism' (on this see Martin Jay, 'The Disenchantment of the Eye' in *Visual Anthropology*, Vol 7, No 1, Spring 1991, pp 27-28).

24 An example of overacting in literature occurs in Des Forêts' opera singer whose performance of *Don Giovanni* ends in excessive self-mockery, screams and unhuman grimaces. See L-R des Forêts, *Les Grands moments d'un chanteur* (Paris: Gallimard,1960).

25 The possibility to direct an animated reality-multitude seems to be a distinguishing point between cinema and theatre. It reflects a monitorable image-processing of time (reversal, condensation etc), the disregarding of which often leads to misapprehensions of film as paintings or pieces of literature (eg S Zizek (1992 (a) and (b)); see also note 6.

26 See Zizek's suggestions on aestheticisation (or 'grimacing') of the Real and the Death Drive in the case of a-historical figurations of Norman's murderous gaze in *Psycho* (Zizek (1992 (a), p 245), of Hannibal Lecter in *The Silence of the Lambs* (Zizek (1992 (a), p 262) and of those in the fear-impressionism of David Lynch's hypersensitivity of reality (Zizek (1992 (b), p 129).

27 An account of *figure* (although in this paper handled somewhat differently) as *matrix* of 'phantasy compactness' beyond the order of the visible can be found in Jean-François Lyotard's elaboration on dreamwork in *Discours, figure* (Paris: Klincksieck, 1971), pp 338-50. See also Rosalind Krauss, 'The Impulse to See' in Foster (ed) (1988), pp 51-75.

28 An example of an environmentalist visual consciousness is found in Herzog's technique of locating the camera in positions of natural human reach. But in *Eudokia*, the camera goes beyond a mere reflection of such realness, revealing its modifying potentials *vis-à-vis* the camera.

29 This refers to all philosophical trends (originating in the Husserlian superempiricist tradition) which, disregarding the complexity of architecture as historical-material experience, develop sophisticated philosophical concepts but, architecturally speaking, naive and simplistic ones; 'Dasein' is one of them. Thus, from Heidegger's *Thing-ing* to the sublimated Freudian *Thing* (Real) there unfolds the Kantian tradition of a priori space, hence a-priorised architecture.

30 Arguing against Tschumi's metaphor, in order to know architecture you don't necessarily have to commit murder. See B T-schumi, *The Manhattan Transcripts* (London: Academy, 1981).

31 An enjoyment traceable on the seat of the 'symptom' (in its full historicity), be it that of the woman and/or spatial experience, rather than justifying an absurd surplusness recuperating and sublimating the paternal metaphor (eg, as occurs in the notion of the 'anal father' in Zizek (1992 (b)), pp 124-25.

32 A term attributed to Gilles Deleuze (eg, see his 'Fold – Leibniz and the Baroque' in *Architectural Design* 'Folding in Architecture', No 103, 1993, pp 18-19). A rigorous critique of the roots of this counter-phallic spatial philosophical expressionism (on the basis of its positive and uncritical rejection of the Oedipal concept) is to be found in Cornelius Castoriadis, *L'Institution imaginaire de la societé* (Paris: Seuil, 1975).

33 Wenders' view, see note 9 (b).

34 For a full account of the concept see Jacques Lacan's 'mirror stage' in Lacan (1977) pp 1-7, and (1988) pp 118-42.

35 J Rose (1975) and C Metz (1983).

KESTER RATTENBURY
ECHO AND NARCISSUS

Architecture exists, like cinema, in the dimension of time and movement. One conceives and reads a building in terms of sequences. To erect a building is to predict and seek effects of contrast and linkage through which one passes . . . In the continuous shot/sequence that a building is, the architect works with cuts and edits, framings and openings . . . I like to work with a depth of field, reading space in terms of its thickness. Hence the superimposition of different screens, planes legible from obligatory points of passage which are to be found in all my buildings . . .

Jean Nouvel

Recently, comparisons of architecture to film has become one of the highest forms of critical praise. Architectural schools are awash with transmedia units full of reference, scenography, tracking and lighting; an exploration of space and time and sequence. Editors of architectural journals have been heard to comment that if they hear another reference to *Blade Runner*, they are going to scream. Belief in the film-architecture analogy, which originally seemed confined to a narrow sector of ambitious architects, has now spread into the field of cultural studies. It is a rich analogy which has generated wonderful ideas and deepened some forms of architectural criticism. And it is profoundly mistaken.

Let's get this straight. Architecture is essentially, inherently different from film. Film is linear, fundamentally linear, an extraordinary process in which the director replicates and subverts the viewers' actual existence, offers them, for a limited time, an alternative way of seeing, an alternative life. It does this through circumstances of extreme control: the darkened room; total attention; provision of object, story, focus, idea, tone, argument, mood, dialogue, background music, resolution. Its creator, invisibly, provides and dominates the experience of the individual.

Whatever architects may like to think, architecture is the opposite: leaky, intransigent, alterable, endlessly subject to total shifts of context, meaning, form, understanding as it is experienced. Paradoxically solid, yet open to such wide interpretation; open, constantly and

helplessly to becoming banal. The screening of a film remains intrinsically special, offering an experience which is perilously close to being repeatable, while architecture's myth of speaking permanence is constantly being eroded by the actualities of the changing world. Film's flimsy substance suggests an ephemeralism it does not really have. A lot of architects' obsession with film is director-envy.

The idea of a special relationship between architecture and film has been leapt on by architects because 'architectural' films reveal and represent architecture to the viewer as architects wish the viewer would experience it all the time. The film's synthesis of observed architecture with time and character, background and mood, plot and meaning, gives potent expression to ideas latent in architecture – and usually missed by the vast majority of its viewers; and it expounds these ideas non-verbally – as architecture is experienced, rather than making a foolish conversion into words. (It is notable, for instance, that straight TV narrated documentaries on architecture are usually profoundly dull.) But the success of film in portraying architecture does not mean that architecture and film are parallel; rather the opposite. In so far as they are linked, it is because they are complementary. Film observes architecture's existence. It is the difference between architecture and film which makes film treat architecture so well.

Some architects – most expressly Nouvel – have identified the visual-imaginative revelations made by the film director as something that architects do themselves in designing their buildings. Hence, for example, the extraordinary, out-of-body comprehension of your own movements and role, as you descend through the pierced screen side walls around the gallery of the Arab Institute, with its veiled view of Paris. The architectural direction is undeniably potent; linking a filmic perception with personal experience of architecture.

This idea has been seized by architects and architectural teachers because it is a vehicle for explorations and explanations. Filmmakers use architecture to stage an idea selecting carefully mood and ambience and view, observing also with a greedy eye the possibilities which architectural space and structure open up. The *Third*

OPPOSITE: Paris through the pierced screen side walls of Jean Nouvel's Arab Institute; ABOVE: Brian Avery's National Film Theatre Bookshop, South Bank, London

Man expresses perfectly an idea of the potent danger of post-war Vienna; also its possibilities for change and surprise: the upper floor window offering a sudden means of escape because of the vast rubble pile of the bombed building outside; the imagined spaces opened up by the revelation than a manhole cover – part of the normal street surface – leads to another system of communication, danger and escape. Greenaway uses film emblematically, in simple expansion of the contrived, concealing significance of proportion, shape and form. *Alice in the Cities* describes beautifully the geographical canyons and outcrops of New York. All filmmakers, can if they choose, make you look at buildings and spaces for so long that you begin to understand them in a different way.

This search for true expression via translation is part of an impulse which is not confined to film alone. In a society with verbal/written language, the dominant cultural form, and a public often described as visually illiterate, architects have become obsessed with the risky desire to translate their subject into a more widely spoken medium. Description of architecture as frozen music has raised its own trail of value and criticism. Narrative in architecture has done much to allow the idea of the individual back into architectural theory, but this transliteration has privileged linear forms over spatial, three-dimensional, material ones. Film, so much more alluring, so much more apparently virtual, has, in its studied relationship with architecture, deepened the cultural understanding of architecture's ubiquitous potency. But to concentrate on the analogy between architecture and film effectively jettisons any last lingering attempt to explore the objective existentialism of the building, to think collectively, politically, historically about architecture itself.

This pornographic reshaping of architectural space into perceived or replicated experience seems to be increasing, with architects nervous and excited at the encroachment of a virtual world of appearances. This is profoundly dangerous. There is a growing body of evidence and argument that our culture is, in fact, deeply visually literate, recognising and interpreting a complex mass of images with extreme sophistication, and that this sophistication is growing with the spread of advertising and television culture. The exponential growth of computer technology is overtaking the idea of a single, necessary linear path of thought with a new matrix comprehending quantum, interactive possibilities. It is not yet possible to predict what new spatial and architectural forms will be generated by emerging new technologies, but in this world of blind flux, an obsession by one old technological form with its parallels with another old technological form is foolish in the extreme.

Architecture needs to have all its forms of perception and self-analysis wide open to deal with a new understanding of the relationships between the perceived and the physical. Whatever the technological revolution will produce or require, it should not mean a degeneration into one long architectural 'feelie'.

When one examines the usual standards of the film-cinema analogy, one finds that it is more of a focused cultural observation than an argument for a symbiosis of media. The Holiday Inn, is a perfect example of a replicated, distributed form, offering a reliable experience which will be similarly encountered, under slightly different surroundings, each time it is visited. But the angle on technological internationalism is not in the normal film-architecture argument. Nor, sensibly, are the crass architectural attempts to describe the film medium itself – like Brian Avery's Museum of the Moving Image/National Film Theatre refit, an appallingly obvious attempt to buy and glamorise the public's self-coercion into a darkened and limited experience. The film-cinema totems are a different, particular expressive genre: *Metropolis*, *Alphaville*, *Blade Runner*; the lure of the eyes into a hallucinatory understanding of the changing forms of the world – Nouvel (the seemingly bottomless, topless Tour Sans Fin); Toyo Ito (the mesmeric room in the Japan exhibition, which seemed to make the very floor level arbitrary); Wenders and Hitchcock; the distanced, dissociate expression of cities and landscapes, spaces and details. They make up a potent observation of the experience of dispossession, of the individual travelling in isolation through a world in which power has become increasingly oblique. That is a similarity in content, not in medium.

Critically, the film-cinema symbiosis is adding to this consensus of spiralling impotence. An architecture fastened on the idea of its own virtuality; obsessed with the beauty of degeneration and loss, a pornographic rather than a generative preoccupation. There is a side of the architectural imagination which is drawn towards this: overburdened with its historical virility and power, and longing to become passive. The prime film quote here is Harry Dean Stanton in *Paris, Texas* talking to his disappeared wife through a one-way mirror peep show window, through which she cannot see who is speaking. It is a masterpiece of film observation: dissociate, essential, disposable, tragic, fundamentally mediated. But for architects to treat this as a goal is a near criminal abrogation of responsibility. The narcissistic reverie blocks any attempt to drag our failing attentions to the still potent, but now rarely discussed political, historical, spatial, pragmatic, collective understanding of architecture and what we might yet still do with it. The idea of an architecture-film miscegenation as the echo chamber of existence is magnificent, alluring and self-destructive.

This does not mean that there is nothing for us in the hall of mirrors. But analogy, description and quotes from films are never quite good enough. One can always draw parallels between films and their subject matter, and they are always an insufficient description. The best experiences of buildings and films go beyond this, existing fully in their own right. Rem Koolhaas' Euralille could be said to operate within the film-architecture genre because of the perceptible way it stages meaning – the city sprouting from the crossroad of European communications – and because of its late twentieth-century distanced, dispossessed style. But Koolhaas' master plan and building never for one moment allow you to forget the solid existence of his building, its place in politics and history. Euralille (and Koolhaas' building in particular) makes you constantly curious about its form, shape and totality, about the things which you cannot see. Chris Marker's film essay *Sans Soliel*, may be a study of Tokyo, but architecture is one of the least important things it reveals. *Sans Soliel* is not just an observation of a different society, codes,

meanings, a different way of seeing and understanding the world. It also constantly reminds you of what it is doing itself, of the nature of its own medium, of filming and editing, of how people look at the camera, of the pornographic nature of looking without relationship or power, of the intrinsic strangeness of film itself.

The most architectural moment in movies for me is in Michael Powell/Emeric Pressburger's *A Matter of Life and Death*. Not the famous totalitarian, monochrome Heaven set, which features in so many parallels of architecture and the cinema and of the cinematographic meaning of architectural spaces, but the Camera Obscura – the beautiful, magical, profoundly strange experience of life itself; the central metaphor and paradox of architecture and cinema. In the Camera Obscura, the room disappears (as does the cinema auditorium), you see life, but at a remove; profoundly different to being out there. It is a smaller and less comic version of what happens later in Heaven. In the film, on both occasions, Powell and Pressberger show that life is different and better. The most significant moment is not inside the Camera Obscura, for all its magic, but the point at which you come out of it.

The ever-changing monolithic urbanscape, encroaching every possible space, as seen in Metropolis, *1926*

FRANÇOIS PENZ
CINEMA AND ARCHITECTURE
Overlaps and Counterpoints: Studio-Made Features in the Film Industry and Studio-Based Experiments in Architectural Education

The first part of this paper examines the relationship between architecture and cinema with a view to establish a context of interest in the world of cinema for architects and, in particular, students of architecture. The second part explores the world of studio work as 'natural film sets' illustrated by experiments with architectural projects from students from the Department of Architecture at the University of Cambridge.

Background

Architects have long been involved in the world of cinema; in particular, in the 20s and 30s when architects were trying to promote the modern movement through the pictures.[1]

This tradition of architects working with film directors has continued since the inter-war period where a number of the great production designers and art directors had an architectural background. Therefore, it is of no surprise today to find that at the National Film and Television School (NFTS) there is a significant proportion of production design students who studied architecture. Indeed, the skills involved to be an art director in a studio production are very similar to those required throughout an architectural education: the ability to draw, to represent creatively a space in three dimensions and build physical models, as well as a good knowledge and grasp of materials and texture, all are essential trademarks of both profession.

An ingenious lighting arrangement, both artificial and natural, is equally crucial to the aesthetic of a film as it is to any successful architectural space.

Finally, at the construction stage, the art director and the production designer need to be able to supervise the construction of the set in great detail, very much like any job architect would need to on a building site.

Reconstructed Spaces: The Case of the 'Man-Made' Feature

Within this context, and arising directly from the creative work of art directors and production designers, it seems possible to argue that the more powerful and the most memorable images of the cities portrayed in the movies come from carefully built sets, usually built in studios which involve a great knowledge and use of three-dimensional geometry and perspectives.

Broadly speaking, most films were shot in studios up to the 1950s. In the 20s, 30s and 40s, the Hollywood studios were at the height of their powers and every studio and warehouse, in those days, were filled with props and antiques ready to be used for the next film. The big studios had an army of people – painters, decorators, matte artists, carpenters, cabinet makers, electricians – on the pay-roll. By the end of the 50s, however, in part due to a much freer use of lightweight cameras, promoted in particular by the *new wave* movement in France, films became more spontaneous, they acquired a documentary style quality and, therefore, were shot very quickly in a matter of usually weeks, on location. In other words, the 60s saw a decline of the studio-made-features. But perhaps one of the best examples of a great piece of building set for a film was executed in the mid-60s in France and is the work of Jacques Tati. *Playtime* is a particularly good example of an architecture created specifically for the need of a film, and it is worth reminding ourselves of the magnitude of the enterprise.

In 1965, during the preparation of *Playtime*, Jacques Tati built a modern city. It was on a vast scale built in the outskirts of Paris. Skyscrapers and office blocks rose from the ground. He literally built working offices with escalators, automatic glass doors, working lifts etc. A few buildings, many storeys high, even had their own central heating system and the site was so large that it required two power stations, which were, in fact, big enough to supply electricity for a town of 15,000 inhabitants

For about five months, a hundred workmen worked on the site. The streets, the car park, the pavements were all laid with authentic materials. There were traffic lights in working order. In other words, it was a full working city. It was gigantic and became known as 'Tativille'. But, of course, it was not just any city, it was the city Jacques Tati needed to explore his idea of the modern city and in order to get the shot that he required, the office blocks were in fact on wheels and tracks and could be moved at will. No 'real city' could have given him that flexibility. In the same way, René Clair recreated in *Sous les toits de Paris* a street of Paris which has often been fooling the viewers as the epitome of the

Paris street. This carefully constructed illusion brought together, in one single street, all the different elements which make a typical Paris scene, in reality, spread out in fragments around the city. But in our mind when, we recollect or remember a city, those fragments merge together. We are therefore entirely prepared to assume that the street scene in *Sous les toits de Paris* is, in fact, something we have seen several times in our visits to Paris. Exactly the same illusion is created in the beautiful sets of Carné's *Les Enfants du Paradis* where the Boulevard du Crime is a complete reconstruction.

But coming back to Jacques Tati's *Playtime*, he had clearly created, with the help of his art director, Eugène Roman, an extraordinary setting which, in Tati's own words, was the 'real star of the film'. And although he never felt that he could criticise directly the architecture of his time, his films and, in particular, *Playtime* are firmly in defence of the individual in the face of a mechanical world.[2]

Of course, the fact that a film has been shot in studios does not necessarily guarantee a great film. But certainly from the point of view of a designer, it is likely to offer an architectural vision reinterpreted through the eyes of the filmmaker. In other words, the film can act as a mirror for architects who can then see buildings and cities reinvented on films. Studio-made movies have also been known to inspire future design, especially when confronted with futuristic visions, such as in the celebrated Los Angeles of *Blade Runner* or the cartoon-like representation of cities such as in *Dick Tracy* or in *Batman Returns*.

Architecture as the 'Natural Studio Set': The Educational Experience

The point was made earlier that both architects and filmmakers deal with the world of illusions. As long as a building is not off the ground, it remains largely in the mind of its creators. Usually, it is represented as a combination of drawings, plans, sections, perspectives and physical models; all attempting and contributing to describe space, street, cities, not yet built.

This world of illusion is, of course, even more poignant in the world of architectural education where architect students very rarely get the chance of seeing one of their projects built. In this second part I look at the experimental work that we do on videos and films, exploring the virtual representation of spaces from drawings, scale models and computer models. They are the natural film sets of our architectural narratives. Those experiments are very much design-led. The architectural representation constitutes the starting point.

The narrative is therefore very much the project. The story line is part brief, part design

philosophy and part aesthetic.

The experimentation is a 'mise-en-scène' of architectural spaces. Film, video in the world of architecture, can help for presentation purposes. But it is not only that. It could also be participating in some ways to the design process and be fed back into the evolution of the project. Or it may even be a preproject enterprise. In which case the students experiment with design ideas, that eventually become part of a project.

Typically, in our experiment we would have a number of 'key players' who would come back as part of a recurrent theme. I have mentioned previously the various forms of architectural representation. So, for example, we may very well use drawings, tracking on drawings, zooming, panning etc. We may use physical models of different scale-using materials. We may use computer models, we may use still computer images or we may use animation. Elements of the brief are likely to be introduced such as site footage.

Another important aspect is the human dimension. It might be actors, it may be passers-by taken from the site footage when taking location shots for example. The human scale is very central to our experimental work. This theme of 'The Body in Space' stems from our continuous work with the life drawing class and therefore finds its way into the natural background, the natural setting constituted by the students' project. It is indeed very difficult to conceive spaces without some form of human scale, hence the emphasis on this particular aspect.

Although the buildings are undoubtedly the heroes (or sometimes the villains) in this kind of experimental video work, we are keen to show how possible, and indeed essential it is to inhabit those spaces. In particular, we have developed a number of animation techniques, computer animation techniques to introduce the human elements into our architectural representation, but in a simplified way [Fig 1]. We are not a film school or an animation school, therefore all the techniques used are very much simplified as all our projects have to be completed in a matter of days, as opposed to weeks or months.

Let us now consider the different ways we have exploited the representational elements in our videos: first of all drawings, then physical models and finally computer models. In each case, those natural architectural settings are inhabited by some form of human activity which helps to bring to life the whole project.

Drawings

Drawings can be very evocative and a starting point for the description of architectural spaces. From time to time drawings have been an inspiration to filmmakers, such as in the case of

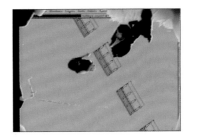

FROM ABOVE: Figure 1, a chrono-photograph in the 'manner of Marey' the 19th-century French photographer (after Rafe Bertram's work on The Swimming Pool*); Figures 2 & 3,* The Swimming Pool *by Rafe Bertram: 'live action' on drawings; Figure 4, 'The body in plan, take 1',* Baptême de l'air *by Bobby Open; Figure 5, 'The body in perspective, take 2',* Borough Market, Year 2019 *by Rakesh Bhana*

Blade Runner where Ridley Scott had been interested in the work of the French comic book artist Moebius. Lawrence G Paul, the production designer on *Blade Runner,* acknowledged his influence on the look of the film: 'The whole concept for the streets where we have video monitors that gave public information and traffic signals was a take off on a little drawing that Moebius drew and we just took it and expanded it.' (Lobrutto, 1992)

We shall look here at two ways of using drawings. First, in section through the work of Rafe Bertram in his video entitled *The Swimming Pool* and then in plan for the recent work of Bobby Open and Rakesh Bhana. In the case of *The Swimming Pool* project, the rendered drawings are first captured on video. The human element is then introduced very much through the use of simplified animation techniques previously described. Within the same picture he also introduces the site location element which is scanned in the background. Perhaps the most interesting aspect of this technique, [Figs 2 and 3], resides in the fact that the swimmer who has been 'frame grabbed' from live action video and who has then been animated through computer animation techniques, has acquired the same painterly quality as the drawing itself. This blending effect, although partly accidental, is used to very good effect.

In general, we found that drawings, and in particular coloured rendered drawings, are a very convenient and effective member of a cast; the opportunity is given to get a feel for the texture of the paper on the screen which certainly brings an extra dimension to the work.

The other experiment [Figs 4 and 5] with drawings was to work in plan, which is of course not so unusual for architects who tend to very much start with the plan; but in that particular case, what is more unusual is to mix live action with a plan. The idea behind this work is to try to bring a sense of scale to drawings which are very often conceived in the architectural mode of representation without any real representation of the body in space, the body in plan. It is rare to see people represented in plans. If there is any sense of human representation in drawings, it tends to be in perspective, section, elevation.

In that particular experiment, we mounted a micro-camera with a wide angle in the ceiling of the University's television studio. The various movements from the actors in plan were then carefully matched with the plan through standard luminance key techniques and recorded at the same time. It has to be noted that this type of technique could be used not just in plan, but could be used to explore the bird's eye view of a building, either drawn in axonometric or in perspective, as shown in Figure 5.

Physical Models

Our students are particularly used to building physical models of spaces which would not only describe the spatial elements, but would also take into account the texture, colour and lighting quality of the material used in their project. We have, therefore, a wealth of 'ready-made studio sets' ready to be shot. Probably the most successful way to use physical models is to use a micro-camera which is small enough to be used in just about any model size [Fig 6]. In the same way as with drawings, it is possible to use the model not just for stills, but for movements for panning, zooming or generally moving around in the model. It is then possible to place it and merge it with other elements as shown below [Fig 7], where a physical model is used as foreground to a very dramatic sky element, very much in the same way as the use of drawings can reveal the texture and grain of the paper. The physical model can show, to good advantage, the texture, colours, smoothness or roughness of the material.

Computer Models

Architecture students, nowadays, are being educated in the art of computer-aided design which they use mostly, in our case, for three-dimensional representation of spaces. The students who therefore take part in those video experiments are familiar with the use of computers and have usually already developed a model of the spaces for their project. Apart from being able to print stills and images, either rendered or in simple forms, they can take the digital tool one step further with computer animation. Computer animation of spaces is still very crude, especially with the very simple tools which we have chosen to use. The colours are often very garish, the movements jerky; however, careful 'digital painting' may also help to create the right aesthetic to a scene which started as a rather crude rendering, as shown in Figure 8. Animation allows the idea of movement in space to be introduced early on, which adds a fun element or a game-like element to the work which is often missing from the studies in computer-aided design. It also allows students to become familiar with the jargon of animation and gives them a feel for the huge amount of work involved.

When it comes to using computer work in our experimental videos, we use single frames. In Figure 9 one can see a computer-aided design representation of an airport space which is superimposed to a frame from a site footage. However, if we use the animation potential offered by computers,[3] it would be in connection with other elements, either from site footage, drawings and, of course, with the introduction of the human element. This 'mixed-media' environ-

FROM ABOVE: *Figure 6, micro-camera in a physical model; Figure 7, use of physical model in* Rough Edit *by Matthew Bourne; Figure 8, atmospheric rendering in* Rough Edit *by Matthew Bourne*

ment is a key point for the appropriate and effective use of new technologies for architects.

Conclusion

The worlds of architecture and cinema deal with representation and illusion; both disciplines can learn from each other. The architects can certainly learn from the filmmaker's ability to represent and move through spaces. We can also learn from the craft and aesthetic of studio-made features where filmmakers have brought a particular vision to bear upon the sets and the architecture in which the actors move. Architects may benefit to understand that their three-dimensional representations are a 'natural set' for the exploration of spaces in movement, which may help to look at one's work in a less static way. Similarly, the modes of representation used by our architecture students, as mentioned above, using drawings, physical models and more particularly computer animations, may constitute an interesting starting point for the film industry, in particular for story boarding.

Digital techniques have already affected, to a great extent, the work and the working practices of architects in a way which has hardly touched the film industry. The world of cinema is still very much rooted in the world of craft. It only takes a short visit to a film studio to realise that, in fact, the techniques used today are very similar to the techniques and craft used in the thirties. One can therefore only imagine that in the near future the cinema world will undergo dramatic changes and architects may well have a rôle to play in the creation of a 'better virtual world'.

Notes

1 This aspect is well documented in Albrecht's book *Designing Dreams.* (see references.)

2 In his own words he used to say, 'the world is becoming one vast clinic but if, to begin with, the inhabitants feel lost, they gradually get used to living in their new town and then manage it, bit by bit, to humanise it by replacing the ultra modern decor.' (Harding, 1984, see references.)

3 Our animation work has been, for the first time this year, entirely digitised using Adobe Premiere on Macintosh computers, thanks in particular to Michael Eleftheriades.

This has been a gradual process over the past four years. Although not quite yet 'broadcasting quality' we are unlikely to 'look back'.

References

D Albrecht, *Designing Dreams,* Thames and Hudson, 1986.

J Harding, *Jacques Tati,* Secker & Warburg, 1984.

V Lobrutto, *By Design: Interviews with Film Production Designers,* Praeger, 1992.

Figure 9, composite imaging: still computer frame over live action in Baptême de l'air *by Bobby Open*

41

DANIEL LIBESKIND
EXHIBITION AND SET DESIGNS

A poorly designed mechanical pendulum weighing a few pounds does not make a good pendant nor does it flatter the bare skin already singed to resemble burnt sienna.

Existence sequence: ur-sanity, fraternity, siamese twins.

The spinning top is shaped through the differential of multiple deformations which, like thought-sections statically reordering the cone's inverted point, propel it towards a dynamically expanding spiral dance that has no nuance or possibility of ascending in parallel segments.

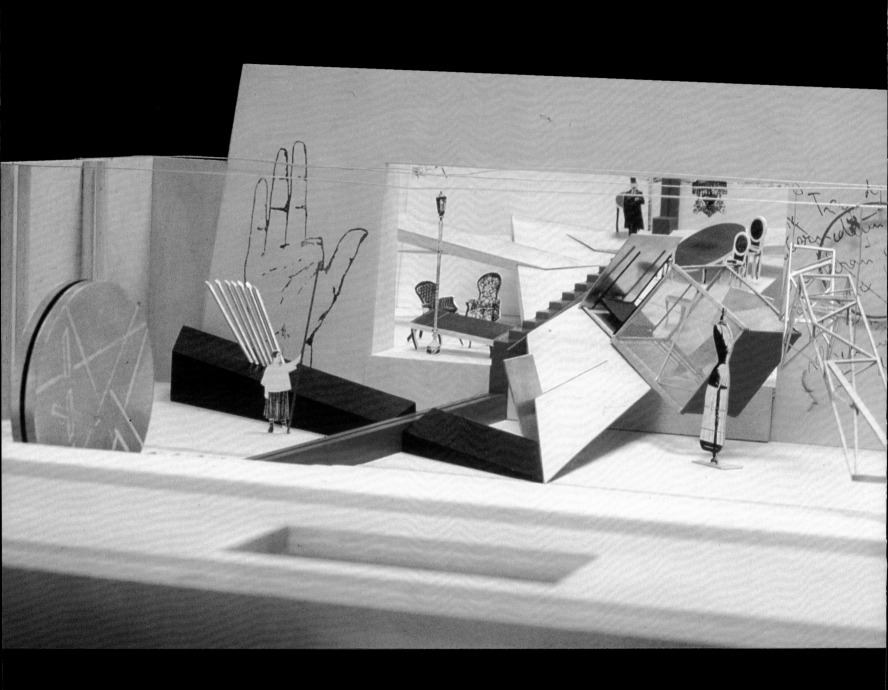

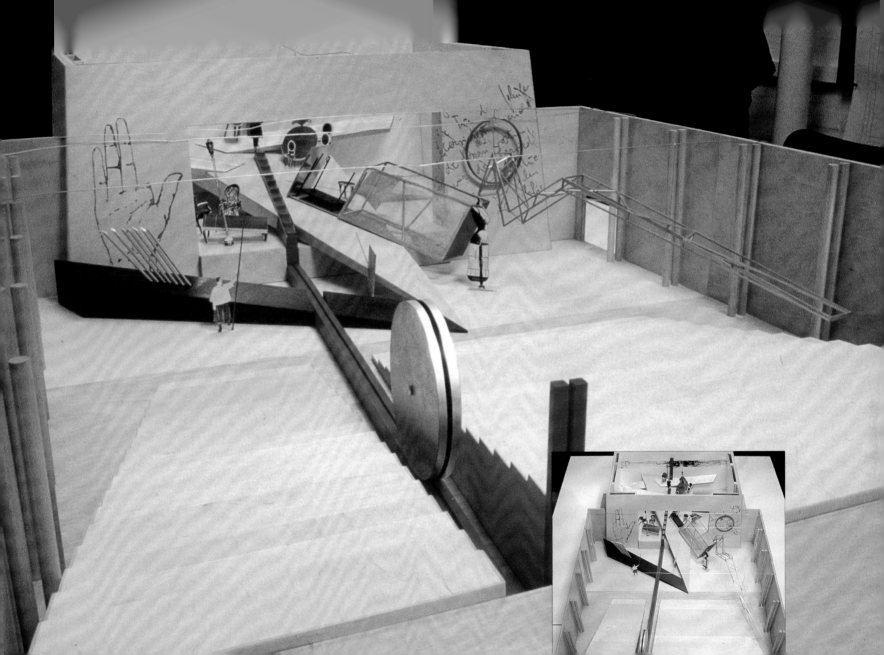

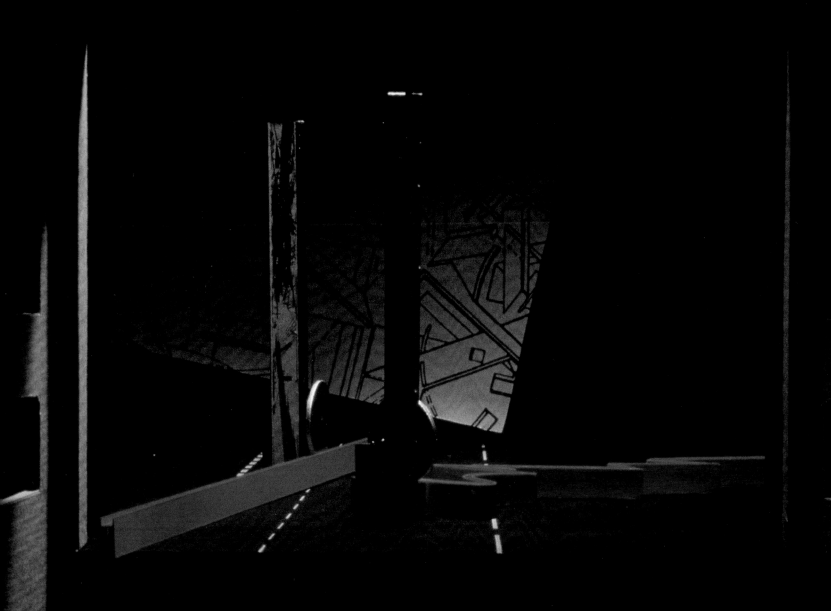

OPPOSITE AND ABOVE: Set Design for
Nürnberg Opera

COOP HIMMELB(L)AU
THE UFA CINEMA CENTRE: SPLINTERS OF LIGHT AND LAYERS OF SKIN
Dresden

A Window to the World

Referring to the figure of speech used by the French film critic, André Bazin, which describes film as a window to the world, the concept as applied to architecture works as a metaphor for the phenomenological specificity of a medium. Metaphor means transference, and what is transferred is not architecture as a whole but only an excerpt (*Ausschnitt*) in the truest sense of the word. Bazin does not refer to walls but he does speak of that architectural element that necessarily

brings about the connection between inner and outer worlds by means of the eye (a door can be transparent but this does not characterise it): the window.

Wolf D Prix speaks again and again of an 'overlapping of space-splinters and media-splinters' to describe Coop Himmelb(l)au's concept for the construction of the UFA Cinema Centre in Dresden. It is no coincidence that he uses the word 'splinter' in this context as it refers to the materiality of glass in a highly concrete fashion. This building material, alongside steel, has marked Coop Himmelb(l)au's activities from the start.[1] Glass, otherwise usually made use of to transparently close

a hole in the wall, defines the outside of the UFA Cinema Centre to a large extent. The central facade of the cinema is windowless, as it is composed of a single window (on two sides of the triangle that circumscribes it) – the permanent production of looking through and looking in between inner and outer.

Coop Himmelb(l)au regards the architect as medium; not in the sense that the building would reproduce the medium (in this case film) but in the sense of ways of functioning that are analogous to all modern media, including film. The practice's architecture attempts to make something visible, to let an inner world communicate with an outer one, to intensify movement and to shape that in-between area, that 'in-between' to which the word 'medium' originally refers to, in this case: the area linking the public area of the street with the intimacy of the cinema auditorium.

How does a cinema that has become a medium in every sense of the word look? The eight auditoria are suspended from the steel structure of the building: four underground cinemas, each seating 200 people, four additional cinemas – two seating 450 people and two seating 500 people – in three transparent storeys. Their material heaviness and isolation act contrapuntally to the light outside shell of the complex – an uneven, multilayered facade landscape made of glass sheets, an aquarium made up of splinters with a triangular ground plan, including eight large, lethargic fish.

Motion and Emotion

Coop Himmelb(l)au is not simply constructing a space containing a cinema auditoria but rather designing a mediating in-between zone, in which the entities of cinema and city communicate with one another: the foyer of the UFA Cinema

OPPOSITE ABOVE: Aerial view of model; LEFT AND PAGES 50-55: model views revealing structural elements of public and intimate space, heaviness and lightness, interior and exterior cinematic projections, as created in the UFA Cinema Centre

Centre is not simply an addition or excrescence of the auditorium but describes, not least through its size, an independent space that has both urbane and cinematographic traits.

On the one hand, the foyer is an open space with ramps, platforms and stairs, a place for encountering people and wandering. A complex structure which also includes cafes, bars and activity areas. This contrasts with the modest cinema buildings of the past decades that, making maximum use of space, used the foyer solely as a channel between street and screen, catering for the buying of entrance tickets and perhaps even for snacks. Here the generous, ramified ramp and stair system of the UFA Cinema Centre attempts to elongate the way towards the auditorium. The cinema-goer's crossing from the rhythm of every-day life that always chooses the shortest route, due to economic pressures, into the flow of time in the film where hesitation, tension and speeding-up are

prerequisites, is reenacted by a two minute walk in which a height of 15 metres is attained.

Karl Sierek states that each cinema foyer fulfils this basic function of linking city and screen in his study, *KinAgora. Going to the Cinema* under the heading *The Road Towards Film*: the foyer 'leads the way and even often anticipates some of that which will follow. Most of all, however, it is part of a new attitude towards time. The auditorium is a time-buffer. The foyer is always an area of latency, that forces one to stand still; a place where one can spend time and kill time: simply a waiting-room.'[2]

The concept for the foyer of the UFA Cinema Centre, however, far surpasses the traditional purpose. One is not concerned solely with a room to wait in but

also with space rather like that outside on the street, encouraging the visitor to, formally or also playfully, walk towards his cinematic fulfilment – Wolf D Prix mentions the word 'procession' in this context. The UFA Cinema Centre's foyer is less concerned with the 'stopping' of the stream of visitors than with intensifying its movement through the space. In this way, the foyer does not fall back into modest 'latency' in relation to the awaited cinematographic experience but steps into the foreground as an autonomous experience of space. The time spent in the foyer is an entertainment before the show – a real preliminary programme, a trailer, as one will later observe – that can certainly take place independently of the film and does not necessarily have to concentrate on the auditorium as goal. Several of the freely hanging ramps do not fulfil the purpose of leading to an auditorium, a bar or some other end but function purely for walking

or as viewing platforms that allow possible perspectives towards inner and outer space, as well as multiple possibilities of viewing.

There can be no doubt that this foyer is not a waiting-room in front of the scene of action. It is actually a space where things happen and are experienced, almost becoming a cinema or theatre itself. This is partially because it comprises, alongside the usual snack-bars, cafeterias and 'sky bar', an underground discotheque. Its elongated surfaces, that are but slightly defined because of their possible modes of utilisation, can be used for concerts, fashion shows and media exhibitions. It is also due to the numerous possibilities for having ever new, strongly contrasting viewpoints, allowing the visitor to immediately become an observer for whom his surroundings, above all due to this change of perspective, are perceived in a new and diverse fashion every time. Coop Himmelb(l)au's demand that the visitor should feel as if he were in a film in the foyer is exactly mirrored in the construction of

cinematographic space. The flat cinematographic image conquers the depth of the space, specifically by cutting and camera movement, as well as by the shifting of viewpoints.

Making Visible what is Otherwise Invisible

By transferring cinematographic ways of perceiving into architecture, a shift in media takes place that is similar to that to which Walter Benjamin attributed new qualities of perceiving art in the twentieth century, in his famous essay about the work of art in the age of mechanical reproduction. Benjamin approaches, so to speak, from the opposite angle by applying the tactile perception of architecture, based both on habit and entertainment, to film:

Architecture was always the prototype for the work of art whose perception stems from diversion and by collectivity . . . Buildings are doubly noticed: by using them and by perceiving them. Or to put in a more succinct way – in a tactile and an optical manner . . . There is, however, no counterpart in the area of touch to what one calls contemplation in the optical sphere. Tactile perception results more from habit than from attentiveness. In architecture it is actually habit that largely influences the

optical reception. (In the case of the Dadaists) the work of art becomes a projectile. It attacked the viewer. It gained tactile qualities. It therefore encouraged the demand for film whose element of diversion is primarily a tactile one that is based on the change of scene that enters the visitor by fits and starts . . . It is upon this that the shock effect of cinema is based . . .[3]

The principle behind the UFA Cinema Centre's foyer is the connection between the sensory perception of feeling and seeing. The whole building is conceived as a rhythmic element within a dynamic space sequence in relation to its urban environment. The inside also offers itself, perceived according to cinematographic logic where focus and perspective changes, where there is a rich repertoire of resting places (*Aufent*) and viewpoints that bring about (*ins Spiel bringen*) stark contrasts of high and low, far and near, narrowness and wideness.

There is also another essential characteristic of cinematographic perception, as mentioned by Benjamin, that can be found in Coop Himmelb(l)au's overlapping of the media of film and architecture. Benjamin compares film with psychoanalysis to the effect that both processes attempt to enlarge our perceptions. Techniques such as close-up or slow-motion reveal layers of the world we perceive that were formerly invisible. The gaze that falls on these through the frame of the 'window to the world' perceives something that had been invisible until that time. Benjamin calls this the 'optical subconscious'.[4] The architecture of the UFA Cinema Centre has similar aims – what was formerly invisible now becomes visible. This does not involve transposing the inner workings of the psyche to the surface. It is rather a process of making the outside transparent in order to allow the interior to become visible. The facade is the window (and therefore no longer has windows) and can be looked through from both sides.

View Out to the City

The cinema is the temple of visual perception and the UFA Cinema Centre's glass facade permanently invites one to look: from outside to inside, in order to perceive the structural relationships between individual architectonic elements, as well as the dispersion of crowds and their movements; from inside to outside, in order to see the urban environment in precisely the same manner as the sky and

…y to night. In the same
lows the viewer to be part
… and of a projected world
… the facade also permits a
…ange of two states: the
… the foyer can experience
…oth an inner and an outer
…e enters this building one
…ndrawing into privacy away
…sphere of a city.
…nds themselves in the foyer
… the city, as the city sur-
…r and continues on into the
…er is a public space that,
…ed by glass and protected
… rain, otherwise stands in
…c relation to its surroundings.
…nctions like skin, like a
…lowing permanent osmosis
…rior and exterior. This occurs
…e area of optical perception
…ne sense of touch and atmos-
…eption – the outside tempera-
…ubstituted by closed air-
…g in the foyer but is reduced

to a pleasant level by the layering of the glass, as well as by storage of heat and cold by means of ramps and stairways.

The foyer is part of the city, framed like a picture by its facade and is no longer separated from its surroundings like two takes in a film that are both separated and unified by cutting. To the same degree that the city remains present in the foyer, the strict demarcation between auditorium and entrance fades away. Film is not only presented in its usual, strict territory but extends out into the whole building. As many as five projectors outside the auditoria enlarge the cinematic experience both spatially and temporally. Space and time before the film is shown become a place for the prelude and the trailers in which cinema is projected right across the architecture. The range spans from movie trailers to works of art by multimedia artists.

The Glowing of the Cold Flame

The projection of the film is thereby largely liberated from its disciplined and disciplinatory restriction to the exclusivity of the screen area. Only one of the five projectors will show its images on a screen in the traditional sense. The other projectors define random areas of the building in the form of picture receivers. The view through certain parts of the glass facade makes way for the visibility of cinematic projections. The films are not only shown in the interiors of the auditoria but on one of the exterior walls the solid material is charged with the fluid lightness of projected images; the third, opaque facade reveals the interior that it hides, namely the projection of films, by repeating this on the outside. The spectrum of cinematographic rays that are scattered in a decentralised manner over the UFA Cinema Centre ranges from the most exterior projection that falls onto the outside skin of the complex from an

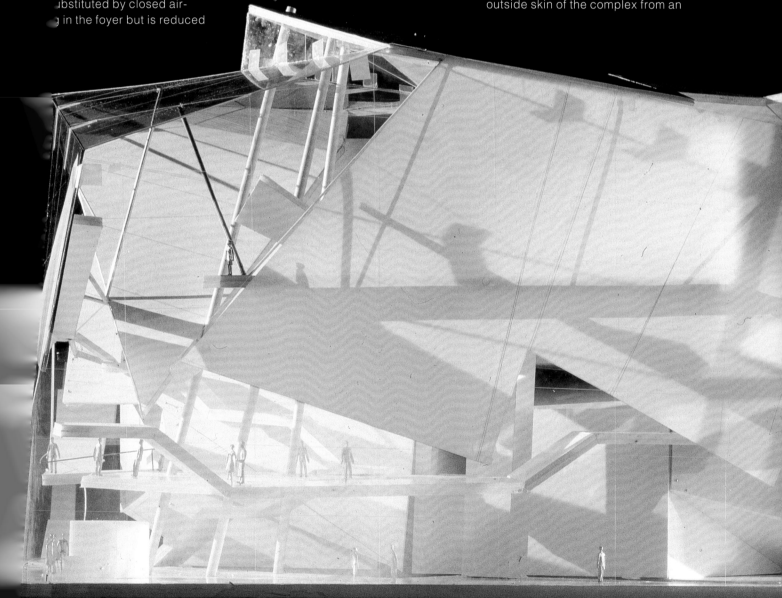

outside building to the innermost projection in the curtained-off, darkness of the auditorium.

In the outer zones the projection and reception of films is no longer subjected to the rigid conventions of seeing and visibility that are found in the interior of the auditorium. The rule that the film image only moves when the viewer stands still and sits at a set distance from it and does not reach anywhere except a flat square facing him from the front no longer applies. The moving images meet mobile viewers that can be close or distant at random, even perceiving them from a multitude of variable perspectives. According to the place one is standing at – on a ramp, when entering the foyer or elsewhere – one sees a different view, perhaps only part of an image or many of these. It is left to the viewer to look behind the images (which would be a frivolous taboo in the auditorium) or to get so close to the projection space that one is more inside than in front of the image which dissolves in details and elementary structures.

The projection rules are structured to create such fragmentation from the very beginning. The rays of light hit a variety of architectural surfaces where screen splinters touch each other and add wrinkles and distortions to the image. The standardised, familiar cinematographic images in the auditorium are contrasted with this new description of the image in the act of projection where the facial landscape of a star receives accents and shifts that are otherwise invisible.

One cannot state that one is disturbing the projection with spatial elements. The cinematographic image has itself become a spatial element and is liberated from being reduced to a regulated tableau with a programmed manner of perception. The image becomes more like the free movement of light in space and therefore can be likened to the unstructured, prelingual state of the purely moving image: 'There are no bodies or hard contours in the purely moving image. Light forms only lines or forms . . . They are in themselves images.'[5] The image is liberated from producing usable values (readability, reproductions) within a regulated economy of perception and can spend itself freely in space. This representation of excess also characterises a large, sculptural spatial element rising up in the middle of the foyer that has

no practical function and serves solely to celebrate this quality: the *cold flame*.

Architecture and film – space and the medium – encounter one another in an overlapping process. Where projected images and buildings meet each other, an architectural and a cinematographic layer overlap in a highly concrete manner. The temporal continuity of a stream of images, resulting from the fragmentation of heterogeneous movements (in 24 or 25 frames per second), meets the building's spatial continuity that interlinks irregular, irreducible architectural elements – spatial and media splinters.

Result: a shining cinema palace made of light and glass. It is not a building with a clear boundary in the manner of traditional cinemas where the window to the world reveals itself merely as a secret opening in which inwardness and darkness turn to light. This is an open body where light shines through, reveals all its depth on the surface that completely dissolves by osmosis with the exterior – it is a body that has become pure skin, and does not simply hold film in its interior but additionally surrounds itself with the luminous skin which is film.

Notes

1 Coop Himmelb(l)au's preference for steel and glass is directly related to the team's most well known manifesto: *Architecture Must Burn* (1980). One should also note that flames are frequently found as formal elements in their buildings (*Hot Flat*, 1978; *Wing of Flames*, 1980).

2 Karl Sierek: *Aus der Bildhaft. Filmanalyse als Kinoästhetik*. Vienna, 1993, p 28ff.

3 Walter Benjamin: *Das Kunstwerk im Zeitalter seiner technischen Reproduzierbarkeit* (1936). Frankfurt/M, 1963, pp 38f and 40f. In the context of shock effects, one should not fail to mention that Wolf D Prix likes to quote the Viennese Mayor, Helmet Zilk (who himself personifies the overlapping of the media politics and television), in order to demonstrate his idea that architecture will be the leading art form of the twenty-first century. Zilk stated that 'there is nothing that can shock people more than architecture'.

4 ibid, p 34ff.

5 Gilles Deleuze, *Das Bewegungsbild Kino 1* (1983) Frankfurt/M. 1989, p 89.

Project architect: Jennifer Rakow/ Johannes Kraus
Text © Tanja Widman and Drehli Robnik

SCHWEITZER BIM

JOHNS + GORMAN FILMS

Hollywood, Los Angeles

A 90 foot high tower dominates the building's modern Art Deco facade; however, the new facility's entrance was relocated to the rear of the building to provide a private inner courtyard garden to enter through, as well as a blank canvas to work with to create an entrance more appropriate for Johns + Gorman Films. Steel framed windows replaced existing storefronts and the line of black granite was continued within the four existing openings. Punched, slab garden screen walls were pulled from the existing building's walls, creating a playful layered backdrop to the new entry. Openings were cut into the existing rear concrete perimeter walls of the building and framed with painted plaster slabs to create definition of the new entrances to the reception area and, up an exterior stairway, to the casting entrance. A veil of steel and glass storefront was recessed into each opening providing protection from the elements, while allowing views into the interior spaces.

The interior is divided into a double height main space that houses the main entrance and reception area, two conference rooms and offices. The adjacent lower level houses the production offices, client lounge, wardrobe, support areas and four large freelance work stations. The upper level houses the accounting offices, a third conference room, an editing room and a large casting facility.

New openings were cut into the existing concrete wall and portions of the upper level floor were removed to allow for views between the two levels. These small, but necessary moves allow the building to function as a whole rather than as parts.

Materials were kept to a minimum – painted drywall, existing concrete ground level floors, new cork tile flooring at upper level, white oak cabinets and furniture and gros point fabric.

The goal was to allow the quality of light to play off the interior volumes and create a continually changing space.

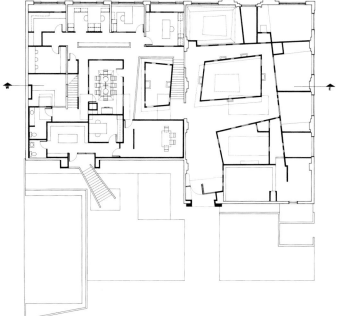

OPPOSITE, FROM ABOVE L TO R: Interior view of client lounge; view of client lounge from reception; view of main space; view of centre conference room; FROM ABOVE: View of main space from upper level; upper level floor plan; OVERLEAF: Hollywood Boulevard elevations; entry elevation; PAGE 59; casting entrance; east-west section; north-south section

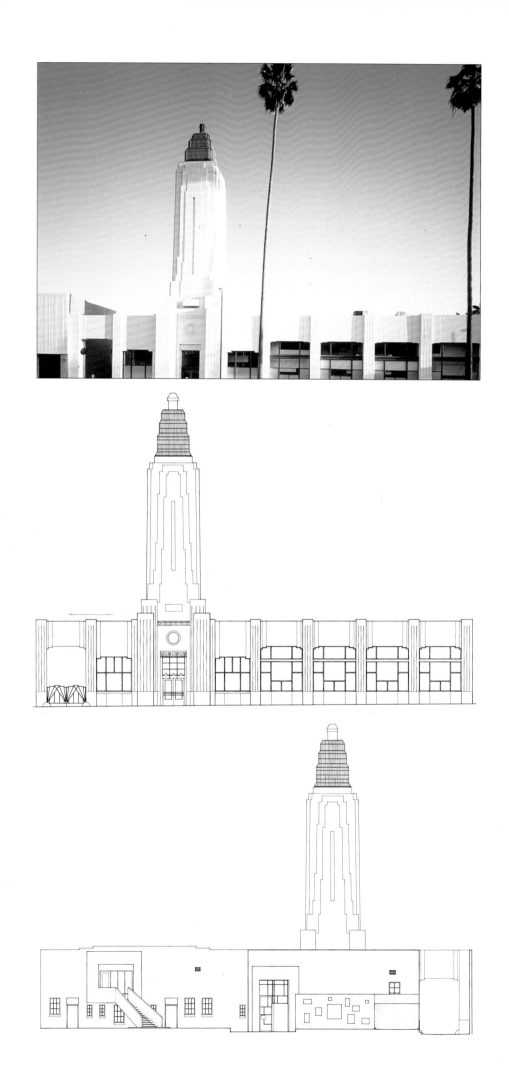

58

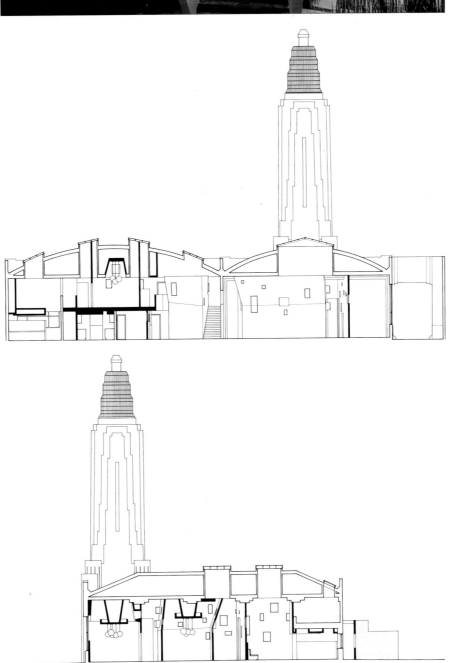

PROPAGANDA FILMS: DIRECTORS' BUILDING

Hollywood, Los Angeles

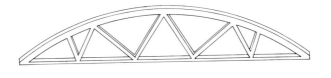

Across the street from the main offices a 4800 square foot facility was designed providing individual offices for the companies and temporary directors and their assistants, a small meeting room and a reception/lobby area.

The offices were to remain simple and basic, because of the high attrition rates in this industry; adjustable to the needs of each individual director for the duration of their stay. The solution was to create a bent and skewed double loaded corridor which leads to an area in the back which could be used as a separate production company, if need arose. The existing skylights were used to play against the coloured walls and trusses throwing dramatic shadows.

The reception area is dark and moody leading into the skylight hallway. The meeting room and offices are carpeted. All common areas are stained concrete.

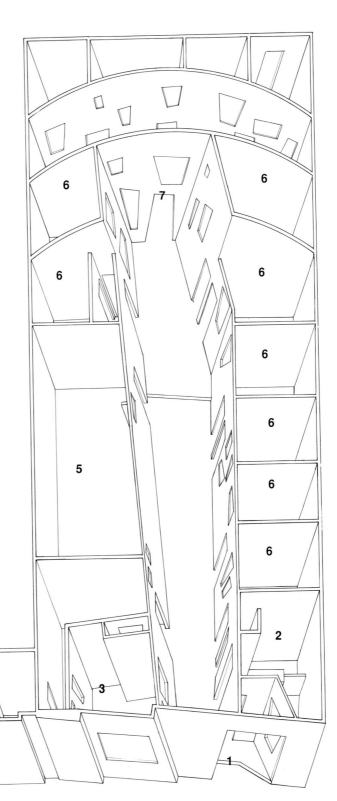

OPPOSITE: Conference room; ABOVE: Corridor view; RIGHT: Plan, 1 entrance, 2 reception, 3 meeting room, 4 toilets, 5 film library, 6 directors' offices, 7 (possible) separate production company area

HANI RASHID & LISE ANNE COUTURE

FILM AS ARCHITECTURE AS FILM
Times Square, New York

Times Square is not only a symbolic centre of a remarkable metropolis, it is also a vivid paradigm of late twentieth-century global urbanism. Here, the city of New York is distilled through an urban montage construed of events and phenomena. Times Square is structured as a cinematic field distorting and conforming to speculative whims of real-estate development coupled with the hallucinatory ethics of consumerism, entertainment and tourism. The cacophony of traffic, information and desire swells in this place of excess and illusion achieving a perfected chaos saturated in misaligned myths and realities. New architectures that are spliced into this territory of extremes can only be faint appendices to an entrenched urbanism concocted from live theatre, fast food, pornography, first run Hollywood extravaganzas, pickpockets, street vendors, preachers and tourists. These and many other vectors circulate endlessly through this frame of difference and delirium circumscribing a constantly mutating city space caught within a complex global narrative. Reverberating effects from other urban epilogues simultaneously enacted in disparate locations such as London, Hong Kong, Paris and Tokyo further distort Times Square's fluctuating dimensions.

Perpetual Encounters
Performance artists and circuses compete for attention beneath the spectacular advertisements that obliterate the sky and buildings beyond the zone of Times Square. Buildings are sheathed in fleeting video images retrieved from both global and local television broadcasts. The surfaces that confront the public spaces are in constant motion making for a liquid-like atmosphere construed of logos, messages and hype. Each experience or event is heightened and made even more vivid within this territory of simulation and transmutation.

Body Shopping
At the intersection of Broadway and Seventh Avenue an oddly shaped glass and steel cage encases body builders and gymnasts whose narcissism and exhibitionism perpetually feeds an incessant voyeurism. This once useless traffic island has been transformed into a veritable display case for the body, which otherwise seems inconsequential within this predominately electronic space of encounters.

TV Free
From the new Broadcast Terminal an uninterrupted flow of public access television is transmitted at the top of each hour. The output from this media centre includes ad-hoc talk shows, self-help discussion groups, amateur video and the latest version of Voyeur Vision. Attached to an exterior wall is a device holding 36 camcorders to be used by people on the street. The recorded comments or events are subjected to random editing within the Terminal where the tapes are processed for live transmissions interspersed into other broadcasts.

Body Surfing
The all-night dentists, manicurists, barbers, tattoo artists, plastic surgeons and chiropractors receive customers endlessly, providing services that promise to soothe both body and ego. The Vacation Salon boasts an instant tan while one of the many Morph Lounges nearby can transform your image into any desired configuration to accompany e-mail messages you might want to send.

Always in Stock
Made-to-order products ranging from pastries to prosthetics are available through voice activated sidewalk vending machines that deliver the goods to your home before you return. As orders are placed, tabulations are made as to the

popularity of certain options and products allowing the information to be immediately forwarded to marketing and census boards. The vending machines also allow customers to comment on proposals ranging from new advertising strategies to prospective architectural, theatrical and other spatial interventions for Times Square.

Love Gas

Meetings and rendez-vous of all genres are available in various locations. At the Love Connect Hotel people sit passively in the foyer soundstalls receiving anonymous voice and video messages while others disappear into Profile Construct Booths. At another location on the mezzanine people are seen circulating about holographic projections of various body parts configuring ideal mates. Some disappear into long narrow hallways where random encounters of both sexes are made. From here, dimly lit staircases lead to private rooms that are bisected by large latex walls. These Safe Spots© are each fitted with personal volume controls that regulate the sound emissions which flow back into the 'meeting' halls.

Souvenirs

The Souvenir Theatres are always inundated with tourists searching for momentos of their visit to Times Square. Among the many items available are sample sound recordings of the space at different times of the day, video clips of angles not otherwise attainable and a vast assortment of miniature re-enactments of events that had transpired before their visits. A large single structure known as Souvenir Tower is situated at just the right location to be a perfect backdrop for photographing and taping one's visit. The Tower's facades change constantly due to a sound sensitive curtain wall ensuring that no two recorded experiences are identical.

Extreme(ing)

A number of structures placed within Times Square contain sports facilities. Here, one can glimpse into the indoor ski hills or the multistorey simulation golf

driving ranges. Stacked basketball and handball courts sit alongside an immense indoor rock climbing structure in a facility that also contains simulation deep-sea diving, wind surfing, parachuting and other E-Scapes®.

Aktion

New films are screened almost nightly and in some cases the actual lots utilised in the film production have been transported to Times Square for the opening night festivities. Smaller outdoor cinemas and theatres are found at every corner playing a seemliness array of repertoire films or lesser known theatrical productions. The rehearsal rooms for some of these street theatres are visible to passers-by, many of whom stop to videotape the repeated dialogues and scenes.

Times Square itself is often used as a film set and the artificial rain machines, spotlights and actors are an appropriate addition to the actual place.

Tableaux Settings

Many of the restaurants and cafes in this area boast perfect views of the Souvenir Tower, and those without actual views have live video feed of it. The street cafes are constantly busy, and some even have rotating platforms that ensure each patron a moment of outdoor seating. In the more expensive establishments waiters and waitresses serve tables while equipped with inconspicuous recording and translating devices that allow them to retrieve orders in any language, once in the privacy of the kitchens or some other concealed location.

Nacht Musik

The Vox-Box is another popular gathering place in Times Square. Here, clients are able to rent private glass rooms that look out onto a vast open space, which could be either a dance floor or a large Group-Karaoke theatre. Special meeting spaces, bars, cafes and Refresh Zones© line a circular trough located along the perimeter of the open space. Entry lobbies have several identity exchange rooms that are used considerably by those arriving straight from their place of employment.

No Exit

Throughout Times Square there are also a number of smaller and more intimate bars and lounges. The most popular bar is the Limited-Time Cafe, which is attached to the exterior of the Souvenir Tower and travels the entirety of its 40-storey height providing dramatic views of the action below. Patrons check into the bar on the ground floor and occupy its space for exactly one hour which is the precise duration of one full cycle of the bar's travel, up and then back down.

Re-lapses

The quieter locations for rendez-vous are to be found in the Silence Lounges that are concealed in various locales around Times Square. Two such lounges are the Cage and the Burrows, both of which are hidden in back alley-ways. The Cage is a small dimly lit space that encourages its patrons to bring their own sound which is played on individual table mounted players and listened to through connecting pairs of head sets. The Burrows lounge is located beneath the ground level of Times Square and descends more than 30 metres into the earth. The spiral floor consists of various seating areas which overlook the gaping void, from which the sounds of underground traffic and trains are intermittently released.

Critical Path

Public artworks are to be found everywhere in Times Square and especially at the space called the Zoo-trope©. Here, artworks of diverse scale and genres are constantly arranged, rearranged and ultimately discarded throughout the day. Often overwhelmed by the immensity of the interior of this cubic volume, visitors can ride one of the many escalators to view the latest works from a closer proximity, as well as from all vantage points. A large liquid crystal screen situated outside above the entrance indicates descriptions of the exhibited works, various critical reviews and corporate sponsor logos.

Hey you, wanna buy

SOFT SELL DILLER + SCOFIDIO

SOFT SELL is a video installation in the entrance of the Rialto, a derelict porno movie house on 42nd Street and 7th Avenue. The project takes issue with the production of 'desire' in relation to the old and new forms of 'urban currency' specific to 42nd Street – such as bodies, real estate, and tourist commerce. Using one of the familiar mechanisms of seduction, the female mouth recites a chain of solicitations to passersby. The voice emanates from a speaker positioned before the original speak hole of the ticket booth.

The project interprets the peep show, another device of enticement associated with the site in order to attract viewers from the street and lure them into a closer look at 'desire'. Each of the four door panels is labelled with an adjective

I'm here for only one thing. The money.
excerpt, *Forty-Second Street*, 1932

Buck: *There's a lot of rich women there. Beggin' for it. Payin' for it too! And the men, they're mostly tutti-fruities. So I'm gonna cash in on some of that.*
excerpt, *Midnight Cowboy*, 1969

Travis: *All the animals come out at night: whores, skunk-pussies, buggers, queens, fairies, dopers, junkies. Sick. Venal. Some time, a REAL rain will come and wash ALL the scum off the streets.*
excerpt, *Taxi Driver*, 1976

We bring a lot of tourists to this area. If not for us, this town would be dead.
male prostitute

The demand for drugs and commercial sex creates street markets that are not about to simply disappear. A handsome profit is extracted from 42nd St's rundown property. A real estate broker described it as 'an ugly cow that gives alot of milk'.
excerpt, 1985 real estate study conducted by City College Graduate Center

commonly considered to be of negative value: *SHAMELESS, SINFUL, SAVAGE, SCANDALOUS.* Each word is just as comfortable on 42nd Street, selling flesh, as it is on 5th Avenue, selling luxury merchandise such as chocolates, fast cars and perfume. Here, the use of base values by popular advertising plays into our culture's moral conjunction of pleasure and degeneracy. A liquid crystal panel is mounted on each of the four doors. As the liquid crystal turns transparent, portions of the large image intermittantly drop away to permit limited visual access just beyond the glass. Each reveals a box – voided of the promised 'object of desire'; simply displaying another single word slogan.

These use an inverse strategy – adjectives of moral principle used by advertising to sell excess: *DISCRETE, INNOCENT, GENTEEL, VIRTUOUS.* The oscillation of slogans to either side of the glass is further convoluted by the representation of each word in a typeface typically associated with its converse.

42nd Street has always been defined by reversible values – an 'unsightly' tourist sight in which the friction between decadence and delight produces a meeting ground of conflicting patronage where, according to the lyrics of the theme song of the musical *Forty-Second Street*, 'the underworld can meet the elite'.

It is a market in which successive forms of 'currency' continually supplant one another: where high-society entertainment gave way to cabaret society at the turn of the century, which gave way to the movie industry in the late 20s, which gave way to popular amusements in the 50s, which gave way to the overt marketing of flesh and drugs in the 60s and which will give way to real estate and fashionable merchandise in the 90s.

Each time, the desire-producing apparatus adapts to accomodate and maintain the new currency. The sustenance of the 'object of desire', however, is dependent on the object's indefinite deferral and ultimate absorption into the mechanisms of its own production.

with Brendan Cotter, Calvert Wright, assistance: Joe Cho, Jean-Philippe Lanoir, Birgit Schlieps

Hey you, wanna buy a pair of tickets behind home plate?

Hey you, wanna buy something for nothing?

Hey you, wanna buy a vacant lot in midtown?

Hey you, wanna buy a second chance?

Hey you, wanna buy an authentic, original, only one of its kind?

Hey you, wanna buy some motherly love?

Hey you, wanna buy an Ivy League education?

Hey you, wanna buy a ticket to paradise?

Hey you, wanna buy your name in lights?

Hey you, wanna buy a new suit that makes you look important?

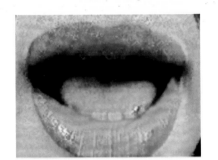

Hey you, wanna buy a rare opportunity?

Hey you, wanna buy a left kidney?

Hey you, wanna buy a judge?

Hey you, wanna buy a turbo-charged, five-speed, souped-up, shiny red muscle car?

Hey you, wanna buy a vowel?

Hey you, wanna buy a place in heaven?

Hey you, wanna buy a one year subscription?

Hey you, wanna buy an all you can eat diet plan?

Hey you, wanna buy a state of the art, high fidelity, satisfaction guaranteed

new and improved model?

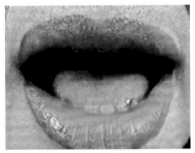

Hey you, wanna buy yourself some more time?

Hey you, wanna buy a brand new baby boy?

Hey you, wanna buy a new identity?

Hey you, wanna buy an unobstructed view of the skyline?

Hey you, wanna buy a time share at the beach?

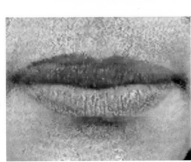

Hey you, wanna buy a memory of a lifetime?

Hey you, wanna buy a system upgrade?

Hey you, wanna buy a head start in life?

Hey you, wanna buy yesterday's charm with tomorrow's comfort?

Hey you, wanna buy the answer to your prayers?

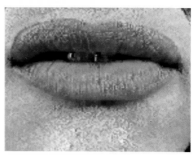

Hey you, wanna buy a one-way ticket outa' here?

Hey you, wanna buy a hot tip?

Hey you, wanna buy the latest sensation?

Hey you, wanna buy a set of encyclopedias with a 4 colour atlas?

Hey you, wanna buy a new body?

Hey you, wanna buy some fatherly advice?

Hey you, wanna buy a building permit?

Hey you, wanna buy a piece of the American Dream?

Hey you, wanna buy a souvenir to show your friends and family?

Hey you, wanna buy the mayor's ear?

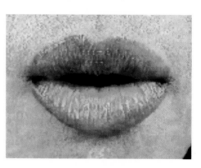

Hey you, wanna buy a deluxe Hoover upright?

Hey you, wanna buy a get-out-of-jail free card?

Hey you, wanna buy your way up the ladder?

Hey you, wanna buy a new lifestyle?

Hey you, wanna buy a place in history?

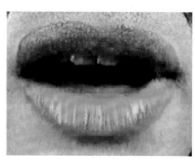

Hey you, wanna buy a 3 carat diamond pinky ring?

Hey you, wanna buy a condo with an all night doorman?

Hey you, wanna buy a sure thing?

Hey you, wanna buy a chance to do it all over again?

Hey you, wanna buy a piece of the action?

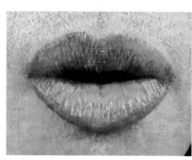

Hey you, wanna buy a place at the head of the line?

Hey you, wanna buy a winning combination?

Hey you, wanna buy a membership to the Club?

Hey you, wanna buy some good luck?

Hey you, wanna buy out the competition?

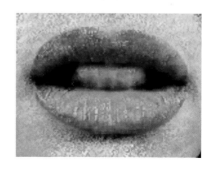

Hey you, wanna buy forgiveness for your sins?

Hey you, wanna buy a good night's sleep?

Hey you, wanna buy your 15 minutes in the spotlight?

Hey you, wanna buy a pair of gym shoes with air cushion insoles?

Hey you, wanna buy an alibi?

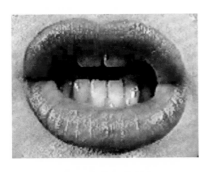

Hey you, wanna buy a hundred shares of no-risk, blue chip stock?

Hey you, wanna buy a spin on the wheel of love?

Hey you, wanna buy a developer's dream package?

Hey you, wanna buy a new reputation?

Hey you, wanna buy some votes?

Hey you, wanna buy the fountain of youth?

Hey you, wanna buy a second opinion?

Hey you, wanna buy your way in?

Hey you, wanna buy someone to take the fall?

Hey you, wanna buy some peace of mind?

Hey you, wanna buy a place in the sun?

Hey you, wanna buy a solid state colour TV in a colonial wood cabinet?

Hey you, wanna buy a piece of the rock?

Hey you, wanna buy tomorrow's memories today?

Hey you, wanna buy some quality dental work?

Hey you, wanna buy your kids the good life?

Hey you, wanna buy a super annuated life insurance policy?

Hey you, wanna buy some classified information?

Hey you, wanna buy a get rich quick scheme?

Hey you, wanna buy a view from the top?

Hey you, wanna buy the hottest ticket in town?

Hey you, wanna buy some culture?

Het you, wanna buy some prime investment property?

Hey you, wanna buy a miracle cure?

Hey you, wanna buy a vacation that never ends?

Hey you, wanna buy a clean credit rating?

Hey you, wanna buy a classic time piece?

Hey you, wanna buy that special feeling?

Hey you, wanna buy a pair of tickets behind home plate?

Hey you, wanna buy a vacant lot in midtown?

JOHN C HOPE ARCHITECTS
CINEMA CONVERSION
Fife, Scotland

Having lived and worked in Edinburgh for many years, painter-sculptors Bob Callender and Elizabeth Ogilvie felt the need to move to the country. They were looking for premises within reach of the capital, which they could adapt to provide living accommodation and a generous, well lit studio space suitable for their work.

The south coast of Fife was in easy access of Edinburgh by road and rail, but, more to the point, the exceptional quality of light with vast sweeping skies and views over the Firth of Forth and its shipping corresponded ideally to the nature of their work and frequent use of maritime themes and materials, including flotsam; hence, the former 1930s cinema on the cliff at Kinghorn.

Kinghorn is one of those Fife fishing villages on the Firth of Forth which, with their beaches and picturesque clusters of white harled (rough cast rendered) houses climbing up from harbour and foreshore, began to acquire popularity as modest resorts from the latter part of the last century. In the early 1930s, to cater for a more demanding holiday trade, a small cinema was opened, fitted out so as to function when required as a theatre or dance hall. Conveniently adjoining one of Kinghorn's principal public houses and an important crossroads, the prominent deep site on the edge of the low cliff rises south of the harbour and commands a splendid panoramic prospect ranging eastwards from the Bass Rock to the south far beyond Inchkeith island up the Firth.

To attract custom, the cinema was built with its back turned to the cliff so that the entrance front, at the west end, addressed the crossroads from the corner of the Harbour Road thoroughfare, to landward. Here, a fore-building harled in the local vernacular tradition but with a requisite medium of Art Deco detailing to flag its cinematographic function, contained box-office, foyer and a corner café, with an upper floor housing the manager's flat.

Abutting it behind, the strictly functional, shallow aisled shed of an auditorium with its hipped roof stretched east to the edge of the cliff.

While the heyday of this seaside picture palace/theatre/*palais de dance* had long since come and gone, the premises continued to eke out something of a seasonal existence, as a café and amusement arcade.

Since Callender and Ogilvie discovered it, Kinghorn's old cinema has acquired a new lease of life. Conscious of the potential the cliff top auditorium could offer them as a studio, if opened up to the light and spectacular range of views over the Firth, they persuaded the owners to sell them the building rather than hang on in the vain hope of a commercial bid. They at once moved into the manager's flat, which provided them with sufficient accommodation to take their time deciding exactly what they wanted to do with the auditorium and, moreover, enabled them to live permanently on site to supervise and participate in the conversion works.

Callender and Ogilvie's vision of the cinema's new role has been sympathetically and deftly interpreted by their friend, the architect John Hope. With a well established reputation for conversion and rehabilitation schemes in both the Old and New Towns of Edinburgh, including the imaginative Scarpa inspired installation of the Edinburgh Old Town Conservation Committee's Offices, Hope was as enthusiastic as his clients to realise the building's potential as their new studio.

At first glance, the auditorium appeared to have reasonably solid harled external walls, the broad span of the hipped tiled roof being carried by light steel trusses on two rows of stanchion columns defining narrow pent-roof aisles of unequal width along the side walls. Of the internal fittings, the balcony and projection box remained at the east end, while across the dance floor – its removable cinema seat-

ing long gone – a now screenless stage backed onto the fore-building, with audience access from the side aisles.

In fact, the external walls proved to have been ingeniously contrived, with timber studding and chicken wire between steel stanchions. Harled on the outside and match-boarded within, the impression of masonry construction looked convincing enough – but it afforded no real solidity, let alone an acceptable thermal envelope.

Taking into account the problems of insulation and stability posed by the exposed site and the flimsy existing structure, the north wall has been stabilised, insulated and reharled, the east and south walls rebuilt in harled brickwork and lined with insulated studding, and a new bedroom, bathroom and entrance lobby have been inserted, with a flight of stairs rising to a generous first-floor living-room and kitchen, where the cinema balcony and projection box used to be.

In consultation with the RIAS/University of Strathclyde Energy Design Advice Scheme, the new fenestration was designed to achieve good thermal insulation while also optimising views over the Firth and exploiting the seasonal play of natural light. Timber-framed triple and double glazing was used for the largely glazed south elevation and for the windows pierced in the east wall, overlooking the cliff.

So opened up and painted white, the former auditorium provides an exhilarating light-filled main studio space. The sheer size of the volume, with the former stage providing a raised working and viewing platform at one end, well meets Callender and Ogilvie's working requirements. A lateral, high-level cat-walk offers an extra dimension, both as an additional viewing platform into the studio and as a vantage point overlooking the Firth. Long disused as a cinema, the converted building now offers a continuously changing kinetic spectacle of sea and sky.

Commentary: Martin K Meade

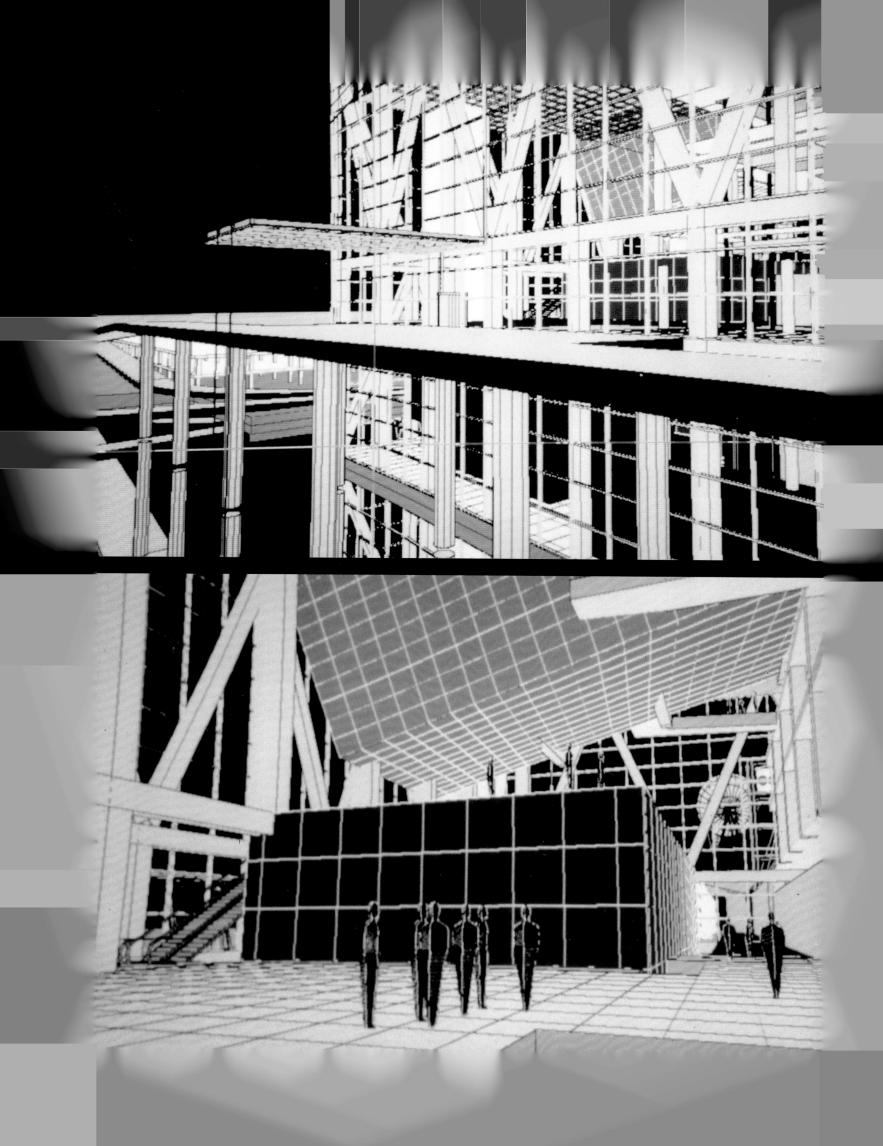

WESTFOURTH ARCHITECTURE PC
INTERNATIONAL CENTRE FOR FILM AND TELEVISION
Bucharest, Romania

The project's challenge was to create an authentic architectural expression for the huge, hypertechnological programme and to be read as a single building integrating all film/TV functions into a split structure, defined formally as the 'Glass Cube' and the 'Podium' – TV studios, administrative, production and post-production departments, a large motion picture studio, an actor's foyer, news studios, make-up and rehearsal rooms, directors' rooms, archive/library, etc.

The Glass Cube is a container for a cross-section of all the specialised structures constituting the programme. The column-free space defining the frontal section of the Cube recalls the spatial features of the TV studios located at its base.

The two office floors which cover the frontal space and generate the Cube's roof are organised within the bodies of the Vierendeel trusses spanning the building

north-south. This strategy allows for the integration of the administrative, production and post-production departments in a single volume that generates large areas of controlled space and reinforces the inter-departmental circulation's verticality.

The Podium is formed by the lower building mass (el +12.60 metres) adjacent to the Cube's north and east walls.

The large motion picture studio roof that forms the Podium's eastern edge is grass landscaped as an outdoor film studio extension.

Within each pair of TV studios, the partition wall can be removed allowing larger live audience productions. While within the Cube the middle studio's wall slides within the structure above.

The Technology Wing's volumetric definition follows the required functional isolation of its equipment loaded rooms. The wing's southern glazed wall reveals the lights of the electronic equipment,

animating the main facade at night.

The Podium is constructed of steel ductile movement-resisting frames, while the Cube comprises a rigid base, an open three-storey hall with perimeter diagonal bracing and two rows of interior columns and two floors of administration spaces housed with ductile long-span Vierendeel trusses. A four-way glazed curtain wall encloses the Cube; a tension-braced glass storefront will be used for the actors' foyer.

Designers: Westfourth Architecture PC, New York. (Vladimir Arsene, principal in charge; Mihai Craciun, Zzing H Lee, associates and senior designers; Razvan Carlan, senior designer; Son Nguyen, Roberto Estorque, Darren Corragio, Harry Chambliss, Michael Horta, Marius Radulescu, project team).

Client: Industrial Export SA, Bucharest.

Consultants: Ove Arup & Partners, New York, structural and mechanical engineer.

BELOW: Site plan

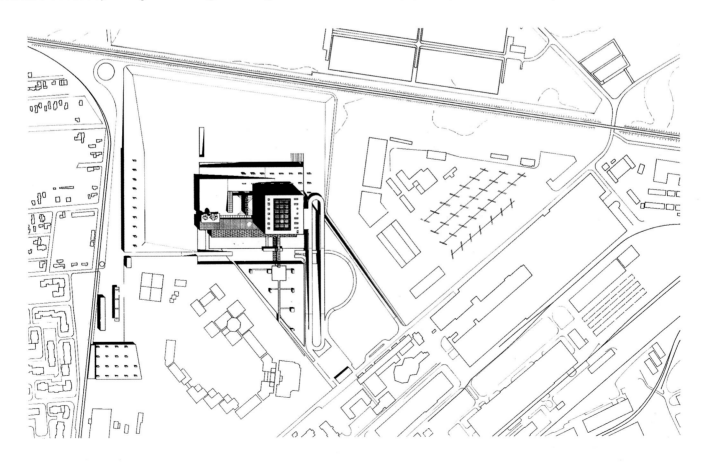

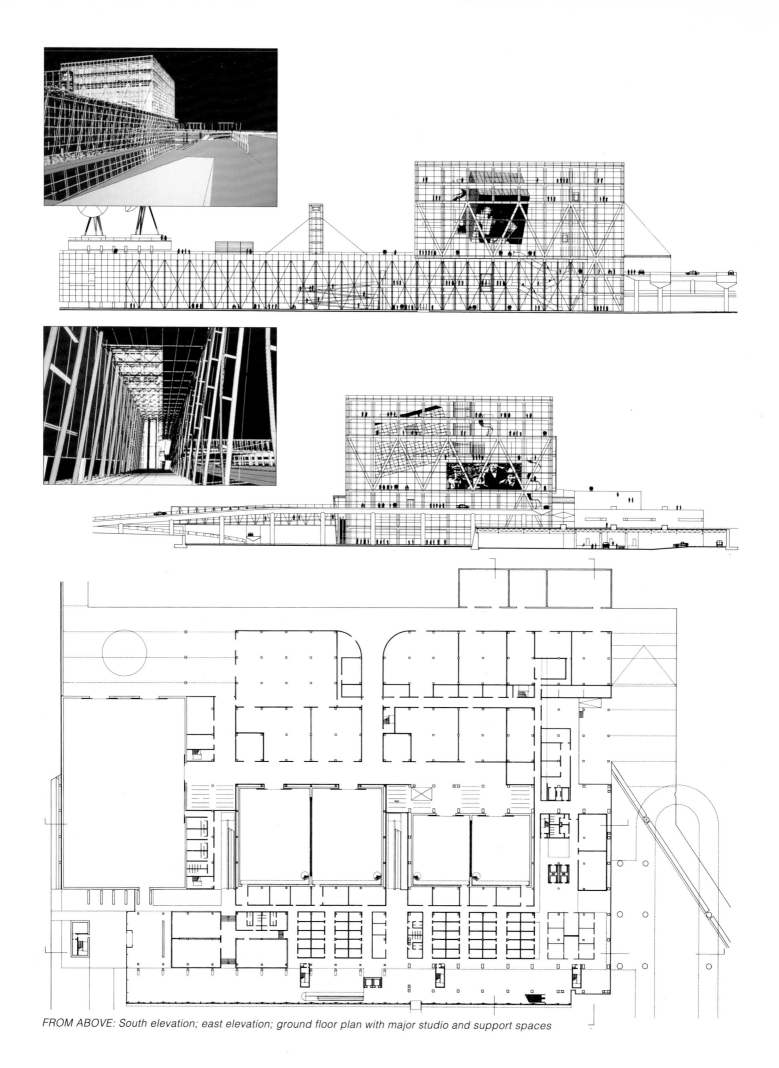

FROM ABOVE: South elevation; east elevation; ground floor plan with major studio and support spaces

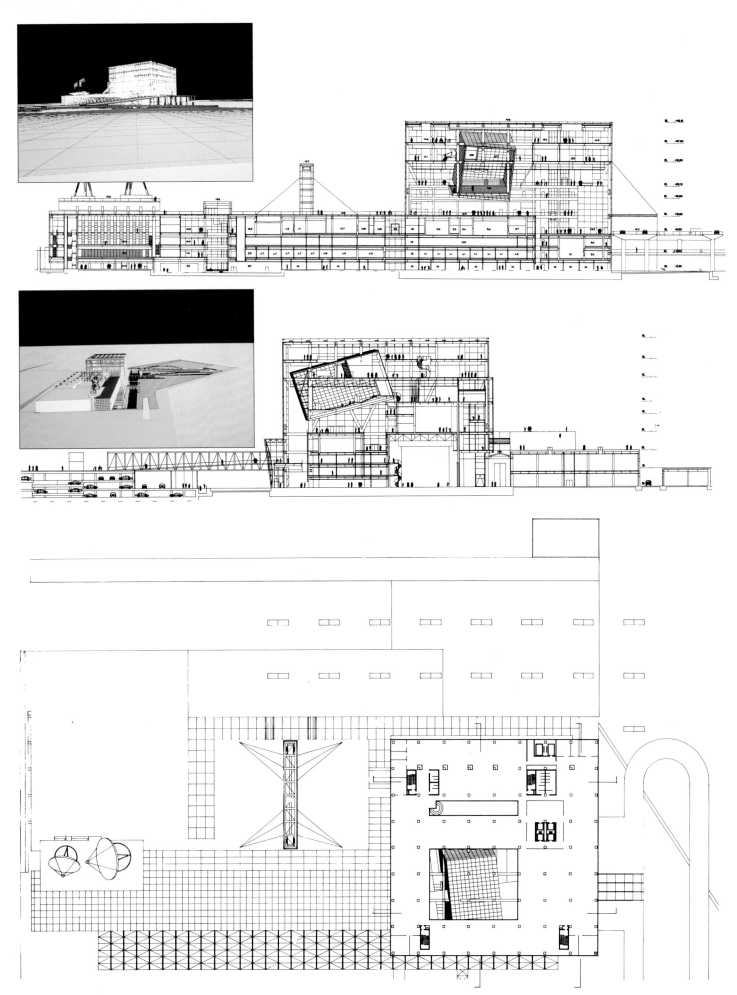

FROM ABOVE: Sections; ninth floor plan with open office

NIKOS GEORGIADIS
OPEN AIR CINEMAS – THE IMAGINARY BY NIGHT
Athens

If one can talk about space-minded films, one might also discuss film-minded architecture in which spatial relationships introduce the film projection – the discourse of the stage – as an organic part of the urban experience.

Open-air cinemas appeared as a summer attraction in Athens *c*1920. People were not obliged to buy tickets (introduced in 1937) but refreshments instead. In the 30s, travelling cinema was also operating, showing at local town and village squares. During 1940-44 the Nazis ordered summer cinemas to show propaganda films. From 1965 to 1975 (the golden period of Greek film production) summer cinema became an increasingly popular attraction among the Greeks. 1970 marked the beginning of a gradual decline, which continues even today; the main reasons were the invasion of TV and the increasing land value in Athens, amplified by the complete lack of any state subsidies.

Open-air cinema established itself as an alternative, local, cheap entertainment, often specialising in classics, comedies, thrillers, detective and science-fiction films, etc. The show allows people to enjoy a classic plot or see their favourite films once again on screen (already seen in the winter's first run season); second time around, the show is open and exposed to the surrounding dense, urban space of housing blocks, streets, squares, etc. Significantly, these films tend to be memorable in terms of their multitude of references to spatial experiences, real or fictional, and on the basis of a classic well known plot. Films are shown for a limited time, three days at the most, becoming brief urban episodes in themselves. The most common type of summer cinema is situated on small, unbuilt sites through which there is direct visual access to the back communal spaces of blocks of flats, of which the cinema soon becomes an organic part. Some operate on existing cinema roofs and, less often, in parks. Seen in daylight, the cinema-building tends to be understated. It takes its shape from the adjacent urban space – only during and via the show at night. As part of

the densely built and populated block, and at close proximity to the surrounding domestic spaces, summer cinema creates the effect of an enacted visual field expanding across a sequence of spaces like those of the street, the cinema stalls, the screen, the rear balconies and private yards, reaching deep into domestic space, from where people at home view the screen through their windows, an extension of the cinema circle.

The Cinemarchitectural Discourse
During the show, the cinema acquires an architectural dimension not only because it intervenes into the city's night-landscape as another urban element but also as it duplicates on the screen fragments of architectural and urban space. The show and the urban experience identify with each other. The spectator holds two positions: identifying with the show and with the surrounding, built environment. As the actual show is coupled with urban space, the ensemble of these two positions constitutes a nonhomogeneous imaginary milieu (a structure).

The cinemarchitectural field is not an expressionist 'space of intensity', but an organised historical-material space. It is not a transcendental, counterphallicly unfolding visual experience, neither does it constitute an imaginary plenitude. It is, rather, the locus of refracted imaginary – a progressing structure of relations of exposure and not an inwardly or outwardly unifying visual expressionism. Such a field is neither perceptual, nor geometrical, nor topological. It instead implies an inverted perceptual field of enacted fragments of customised space, a Merleau-Pontian *flesh* critical to the Bergsonian continuum, resisting the hyper-realist space of TV. City-profiles are not overlapping or unfolding (in a collage or counter-collage fashion), but are articulated one-by-one in real proper shapes providing a spatial accuracy which does not simulate but manipulates the accidental. The spectator's impressions cannot be sustained by any ocular consciousness. The proposed

Project team: research and image design: Nikos Georgiadis, Costas Kakoyiannis, Tota Mamalaki; photographer: George Vrettakos; computer processing: Vaios Zitonoulis

imaginary field does not assimilate vision, neither does it expand or trick the visual; but re-synthesises it to introduce a lack within the visual, as the plot now becomes the latter's vanishing point, a missing desired object within the visual. It sets up an analytic state of affairs for both directions: cinema show and city.

The Plot-Object

There is no definite form for a story, all scenarios can be re-defined as requested on the enacted visual field which engenders a whole new world of possible, as yet unwritten, scenarios, episodes, characters from the past and the future, addressed either to the film or the city. The literary aspect is demystified but not popularised. To people going

to see films for a second time, the plot is no longer a story that attracts because of its complexity; as they say they 'know the plot' already. In summer, the film survives as a pure plot worth experiencing again and again; *enjoyment* arises in the course of such a repetition as the plot becomes a lost-and-found, a communicable object of desire on the plane of spatial experience. Here is a *spatial thriller*, an inverted *folie* perhaps; not a formless, uncanny, abyssal and monstrous or decomposed space, but an overformed, customised, enjoyable and composing one. Surely, a potential transferential field opens. The film is to be seen twice; so is the city.

Watching Both Directions

The show 'as' city: watching from the show to

the city, the spectator, already familiar with the wholistic manner of the plot-bind of the film viewed, can easily identify with the surrounding environment in terms not of fragmented space but of integrated wholes: domestic universes, settings of space, views of the city, etc. The plot is missing and quested on the locus of the Other (the city) as symbolic law of a general character. A new symbolic law for the city is requested, the spectator becomes the city's legislator. *The city 'as' show*: watching from the city to the show, the man on the street can identify with the show from afar, he can register not

with the film as a whole but with fragments of envisioned space, snaps of episodes already familiar to the discontinuous structure of urban reality. The plot as local episode is missing and quested on the locus of the Other (the show). New ideas for film-episodes are requested, the citizen becomes film-director.

The surrounding architecture becomes a paradox of the show. It transfers the audience onto the discourse of the filmable object: the real city (the discourse of reality) which conditions interest and attraction even for simplistic plot-minded films which perhaps are not worth seeing at all. Also, the show becomes a paradox of architectural experience transferring the city episode onto the discourse of the urbanised visual art: the

real position of the show and the filming camera (as ability of directing vision and imagery) which enables conditions of envisioning, applied even to unliveable cities, cities which, perhaps, are worth leaving.

Imaginary Duplications

– The city's unbuilt space between dwellings, the real negative space, back as opposed to front, meets the mysterious underworld space of the detective film.
– The local universe, spatial ideal of the limited but overcrowded, imploding domestic space meets the ideal space, the hyperdimensional expanding universe of Sci Fi.
– The immobile but pulsating heterogeneous urban space meets the homogenised back-ground action space in motion of the

adventure film.
– The ordinary, safe and overdomesticised dwelling space meets the dark unhomely spaces of the horror movie.
– The wide-open, extrovert lit rear windows meet Hitchcock's *Rear Window* and the unhappy doors and staircase landing of Norman's house in *Psycho*.

As we watch the film, all those balcony doors, safe and self-conscious in the night, moderately visible, are themselves looking at us a bit longer than a disrupting menacing gaze would last, exposing our literary-minded voyeurism, while possible new scenarios arise for better film or city making. Perhaps, paraphrasing Lacan, the Unconscious could indeed look at us a little more, provided we are prepared to devisualise it.

BRIAN AVERY

IMAX CINEMA

South Bank, London

The National Film Theatre (NFT) propose siting a wide view screen, 500-seat cinema in the centre of the Bull Ring, named the IMAX Cinema. This is identified as a new gateway to the South Bank Centre, London, providing a link with the existing Museum of the Moving Image (MOMI), and the NFT facilities alongside and under the Waterloo Bridge. The building would be of six storeys with a raised foyer at first-floor level.

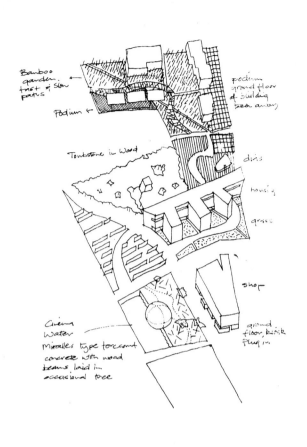

Bamboo
garden.
roof of slow
paths

Podium +

Tombstone in Wood

podium
ground floor
of building
seen away

dins

housing

grass

shop

Green
water
Moralles type forecout
concrete with wood
beams laid in
occasional tree

ground
floor brick
Plug in

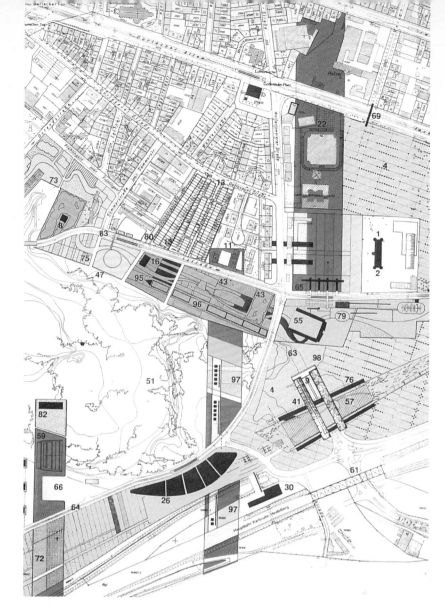

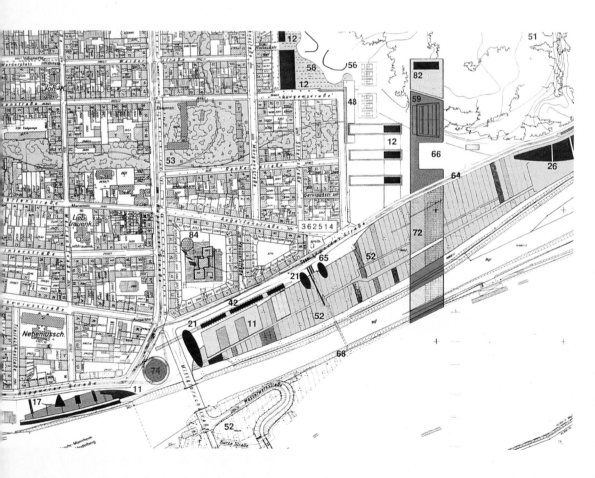

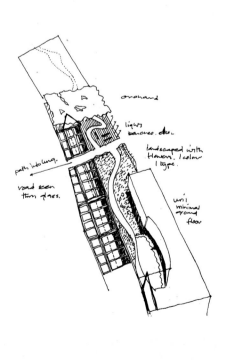

orchard

lights
barriers etc

landscaped with
flowers. 1 colour
1 type.

path including

road seen
through glass

uni
minimal
ground
floor

DOMINIC PAPA AND JONATHAN WOODROFFE

FADE IN FADE OUT

Karlsruhe, Germany

Who can deny that the advent of film and other visualising techniques have had a dramatic impact on our perception of the environment. At the same time, it seems clear that traditional urban models seem no longer appropriate, or are in fact inadequate to deal with the contemporary urban condition.

The very nature of urbanism is changing. A diffused geography of late capitalism, intensified sociopolitical conflicts and the globalisation of these unseen forces is redefining urban programme and the use of space within the city.

Furthermore, the development of image seduction, of computer simulation and virtual space continues to question our expectations and aspirations of the city while simultaneously suggesting exciting new potentials.

Within this context, how can contemporary techniques of film/video contribute

positively to this emerging urbanism? Sergei Eisenstein's techniques of frame and montage, Oskar Fischinger's abstract forms and colour patterns and Jean-Luc Godard's reversals suggest alternative modes of operation. Architecture and programme can be viewed as frame or framing devices of an urban scenario that can be turned on or off, phased, made fluid or morphed, each autonomously according to site specificity and changing urban conditions. Cut, spliced and superimposed, urban strategies should stimulate a multiplicity of events and readings of the city.

Similarly, our increased mobility, whether it is the spectator moving through space or, more recently, TV space moving past the stationary spectator, begins to re-affirm the cognitive mapping described through the itinerary, the act of 'derive' or drifting, established by the 'Situationists' in the 1950s.

The project for Karlsruhe acknowledges these two contemporary phenomena in a search for an urbanism that can be catalytic through the identification of specific sites, events and programmes, in order to act as foci for urban intervention. No longer fascinated by what the framed image expresses but what it is capable of doing, the omnipotence of the traditional master plan is rejected in favour for a form of city space based more on a strategy of enabling where experience and meaning becomes, as in film and video, cumulative allowing us to effortlessly project our desires, fears and aspirations.

Studio 333 in collaboration with Evzen Novak and Simon Dodd. International Ideas Competition for Southeast Karlsruhe, Gottesaue, Bundesgartenschau 2001, Germany.

OPPOSITE: Representations of the city fabric

DISNEY
REALITY-FILM-REALITY TRANSFERENCE

Spaceship Earth, the Chinese Theatre, Toon Town, the Sleeping Beauty Castle, Discoveryland, the list is endless. Yet all the environs found in Disneyland, Disney World and EuroDisney encapsulate the whole notion of transferring what is found in reality, or the reality to be, to the filmic space and then onto the world of Disney. What is achieved is the essence of film, not 'just a set, but a living, breathing, three-dimensional "cartoon" environment. Everything is exaggerated . . . to convey the (filmic) elements . . . no straight lines or conventional architecture'.

Architecture from around the world, from the real space time of the past and present, is adapted (over exaggeration, brighter colours) and assigned to cinema, to the ever-lasting filmic space. Such a physical and mental transfer creates an 'unreal', imaginary element. This element becomes heightened as it returns to the natural surroundings of the theme parks; not as the original studied building but as the exaggerated construction. The imagined is confronted with reality and reality with the imagined; two dimensions with three dimensions; the fantasy with the everyday.

One is able to escape into the 'real-filmic' space, enjoy themselves and act out their fantasies. The magic of film comes to life. Cinematic architecture and solid, tangible architecture are brought together within the confines of exclusive hideaways.

LORCAN O'HERLIHY
ARCHITECTURE AND FILM

The narrative potential of film suggests a strong bond with the novel. Film and the novel tell 'spatial stories' from the perspective of a narrator. As with theatre, architectural construction can be perceived as part of a performance. The idea that the movement of a body through a constructed space and participating in its narration lends itself to a more intimate union between film and architecture.

There has been a reemergence of interest in film in critical and theoretical work on the relationship between space and visual representation.

MONTAGE

The implications of cinematic language (frame, montage, illusion, movement-image, cut, scene) have a dialectical relationship to the tectonics of building. Montage includes devices such as recurrence, inversion and substitution, which suggests an architecture of collision, a principle established by Sergei Eisenstein in dialectical opposition to Pudovkin's theory (for Pudovkin, montage was 'the method which controls the psychological guidance of the spectator').

Bernard Tschumi realised these ideas in his La Villlette Project:

... la Villette ... substitutes an idea comparable to montage ... In film, each frame is placed in continuous movement ... The park is a precise set of architectonic, spatial or programmatic transformations. Contiguity and superimpositions of cinegrams are two aspects of montage. Montage ... includes inversion, substitution and insertion ... whereby invention resides in contrast – even in contradiction.

Montage also suggests that two film pieces of any kind, placed together, combine into a new concept, a new quality, arising out of that juxtaposition. This is specific not only to cinema but is met with in most examples where we have to deal with juxtapositions of two phenomena.

FRAMING

Framing is the art of choosing the parts of all kinds which become part of a set. This set is a closed system, relatively and artificially . . . and,

determined by the frame, can be considered in relation to the data it communicates . . . it is 'informatic' and saturated or rarefied . . . It is an optical system when it is . . . in relation to the point of view, to the angle of framing . . . Finally, it determines an out-of-field, sometimes in the form of a larger set which extends it, sometimes in the form of a whole into which it is integrated.
Deleuze

The architecture of the frame celebrates specular space and acknowledges blind space. Film succeeds when we are held between these spaces.

The limitations that are imposed by the frame and the composition of the image within the frame are important aspects. As is the relationship between the movement of the camera and the movement within the frame.

The filmmaker composes in three dimensions and three sets of compositional codes: the geography of the space to be photographed; the plane of depth perception; and the plane of the image.

These filmic techniques (compositional codes) suggest parallels to architectural composition in space. Film is concerned with the plane of the image, the architect with the point of view of the body within three-dimensional space. In 'Montage and Architecture' Sergei Eisenstein argues that in the transition from real to imaginary movement, architecture is film's predecessor. He sets out this position, contrasting two 'paths' of the spatial eye: the cinematic, where a spectator follows an imaginary line among a series of objects, through the sight as well as the mind and the architectural.

How the architect works with a shape, form, light, balance, colour, movement and expression within the geography of space and depth is how architecture manifests itself.

Film is considered a phenomenon very much like language. As there is no specific rule of usage it cannot be argued that it is a language system like written/spoken language. In the last half of the century, film theorists have described a rational and scientific structure for film and it is in this area that architects have ventured, in search of new ways to celebrate architecture through space and time.

Bibliography

David Bordwell, *Narration in the Fiction Film.*
Gille Deleuze, *Cinema I: The Movement-Image.*
Sergei Eisenstein, *The Film Sense.*
Bernard Tschumi, *Cinegramme folie le Parc de la Villette.*

James Monaco, *How to Read a Film.*
Anthony Vidler, *The Explosion of Space: Architecture and the Filmic Imaginary.*

OPPOSITE: Venice Production Office, 1992

O'HERLIHY + WARNER ARCHITECTS
VIDEO PRODUCTION OFFICE

Charged with renovating a 350 square foot storefront space in Venice (Los Angeles) to house a video production office, the architects sought an architectural interpretation of the two-dimensional nature of film, the circumscribed vision of the camera and the frame-by-frame possibilities of the editing process. The design is a 'landscape of singular elements' emphasising surface treatments and sets up disparate 'scenes' on opposing sides of the space.

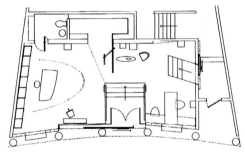

LORCAN O'HERLIHY ARCHITECTS
ISLE OF MAN

The project is located on the north-west point of the Isle of Man (situated off the north-west coast of England) encountering panoptic views of Ireland and Scotland. The house sets up a series of *mise-en-scéne* (as opposed to creating obvious relationships with the ocean vistas) linked by a cinematic ramp on which one passes through the house. The house both blocks and exposes the framed views. By virtue of the framing possibilities of the editing process, the programme is inverted (the kitchen is the embryonic stage of the journey) to create an architecture which contains the element of surprise.

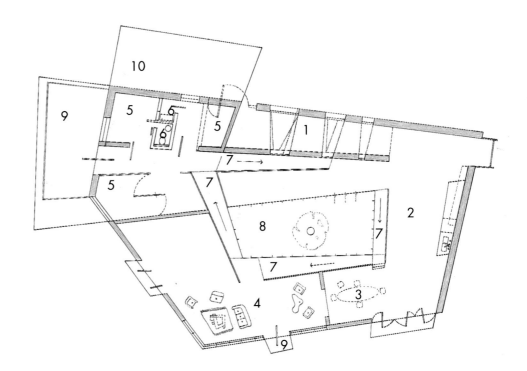

ABOVE: Plan: 1 entry gallery; 2 kitchen; 3 dining; 4 great room/living room; 5 bedrooms; 6 bathrooms; 7 cinematic ramp; 8 courtyard; 9 viewing deck; 10 studio/editing room below; BELOW: Elevation: showing materials used in construction: clear glass, translucent glass, stone, colour plaster and pilotis

LORCAN O' HERLIHY

ARCHITECTURE AND CINEMA

The Architectural Association, London

The two projects assigned this year tested ideas and developed the students' ability to think through architecture. The work introduced architecture as the constructed spatial relationship between human bodies, the object and the landscape. Students explored the relationships between the tectonics of building and site, the primary architectural programme, the making of space and perceptual and spatial cinematic phenomena. These cinematic phenomena acted as a foil for invention in creating architectural construction and experience.

The elements of cinematic language – scene, montage, frame, cut, movement-image, illusion and depth of field have a dialectical relationship to the tectonics of building. The technique of montage includes devices such as recurrence, inversion, recombined images and substitution, which suggest an architecture of rupture. The framing principle allows the many parts of a sequence of spaces in a building to be infinitely combined, superimposed, like the cine-grams of a film.

Like cinema, construction possesses an inherent order and logic which has a direct impact on form, in terms of dimension, density, structure and materiality. The relationship between the nature of the materials and the method of assembly constitutes the tectonics of building, which are tied to the concept of space.

The first project was a critical discourse on the abolition of the privileged and hierarchical relationship between the spectator and the spectacle, author and reader, viewed and viewer. This collapsed and violated boundary became the site for a *theatre* of action.

The second project was the design of a *cinema*. As part of our research we conducted a screening of the filmmakers Eisenstein, Antonioni, Fellini, Greenaway, Wenders, Resnais and Fritz Lang; to analyse whether the narrative mode of cinema paralleled architectural/spatial narration.

Cinema Venezia 94

An open air cinema is to be designed for the Venice Film Festival 94. The site is off Canale Giudecca along the Zattere. The platform (site) will act as a cinema for the duration of the film festival and as an additional customs drop off point at all other times. Cinema Venezia 94 attempts to look at the apparatus free from the constraints of the stereotype.

The real becomes spectacle or spectacular, and fascinates for being the real thing. The everyday is identified with the spectacular. Fellini achieves the deliberate confusion of the real world and the spectacle by denying the heterogeneity of the two worlds, by effacing not only distance, but the distinction between the spectator and the spectacle.
Barthélémy Amengual

Students: Urs Britschgi, Najlaa El-Ageli and Oliver Domeisen

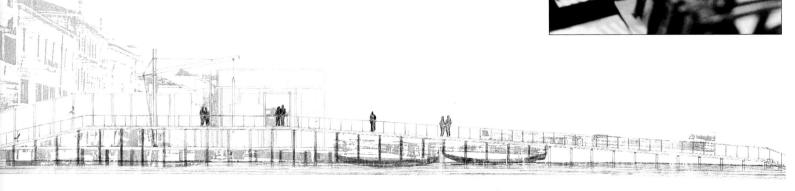

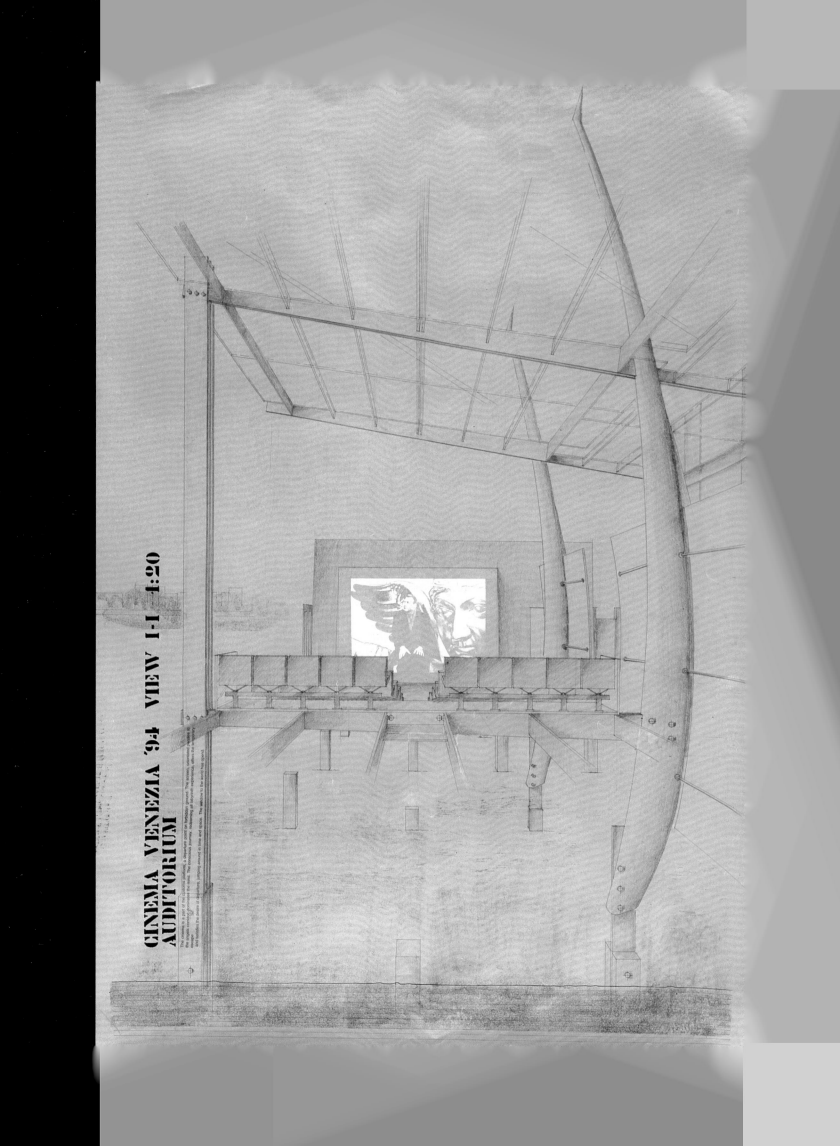

CINEMA VENEZIA '94 VIEW 1-1 1:20
AUDITORIUM